SOCIAL SECURITY
for Everyone

2021–2022 Edition

SOCIAL SECURITY
for Everyone

2021–2022 Edition

CARL W. BATTLE

ATTORNEY-AT-LAW

ALLWORTH PRESS
NEW YORK

Allworth Press books may be purchased in bulk at special discounts for sales promotion, corporate gifts, fund-raising, or educational purposes. Special editions can also be created to specifications. For details, contact the Special Sales Department, Allworth Press, 307 West 36th Street, 11th Floor, New York, NY 10018 or info@skyhorsepublishing.com.

25 24 23 22 21   5 4 3 2 1

Published by Allworth Press, an imprint of Skyhorse Publishing, Inc. 307 West 36th Street, 11th Floor, New York, NY 10018. Allworth Press® is a registered trademark of Skyhorse Publishing, Inc.®, a Delaware corporation.

www.allworth.com

Library of Congress Cataloging-in-Publication Data is available on file.

Cover design by Mary Belibasakis King

Print ISBN: 978-1-62153-781-6
eBook ISBN: 978-1-62153-782-3

Printed in the United States of America

TABLE OF CONTENTS

INTRODUCTION

Almost every person in the United States is either paying Social Security taxes or getting Social Security benefits—or is closely related to someone who is. While many of us associate Social Security primarily with retirement, it also provides, among other things, vital income to families of workers who are disabled or who die before retirement age. More than 60 million Americans receive some form of Social Security benefit. That figure represents about one out of every six Americans.

The Social Security System, created under the Social Security Act of 1935, was comprehensive in scope and designed to "provide for the general welfare." It covers a broad range of programs, including retirement insurance, disability insurance, survivor's insurance, hospital and medical insurance for the aged and disabled, black lung benefits, Supplemental Security Income (SSI), unemployment insurance, and varied public assistance and "welfare" services. This book will focus primarily on the "typical" Social Security benefits such as retirement, disability, and survivor's benefits.

There is no doubt that Social Security establishes an important foundation of retirement protection for nearly every American, and there are a lot of positive features of its benefits. These positive features of Social Security include i) guaranteed and defined payments, ii) progressive benefits based on the level of earnings history, iii) payments which increase based on the US inflation rate, iv) benefits which are safe from the risks of the stock market and other investment channels, v) income which is not based on level of wealth, and vi) an income base designed to keep the typical American retiree above the US poverty level.

Social Security is one of few options for receiving a guaranteed and defined retirement benefit for most Americans. Many employers have shifted from offering traditional defined-benefit pension plans (which guarantee a certain benefit level upon retirement) toward defined-contribution plans such as 401(k)s. These defined-contribution plans only pay a benefit based on a worker's or employer's contributions into the plan and the rate of return they earn. This means that Social Security will be most workers' only source of guaranteed, lifetime retirement income.

Social Security benefits are progressive in their effect, because they represent a higher proportion of a worker's prior earnings for those workers making lower earnings. The result is that someone (retiring at age 65 in 2020) who earned about 45 percent of the average US wage will have a Social Security retirement benefit which replaces about half of his or her prior earnings. However, the Social Security retirement benefits for high earners (with about 160 percent of the average US wage) replace about one-third of their prior earnings. Social Security benefits are based on the earnings on which you pay Social Security payroll taxes. The higher your earnings are (up to the current maximum taxable amount of $137,700), the higher your Social Security benefit will be.

Once you start receiving Social Security, your benefits increase to keep pace with inflation. This important feature helps to prevent people from falling into poverty as they get older. This is a major difference from most private pensions and annuities which are not generally adjusted for inflation.

Your Social Security benefits are free from the general uncertainties and speculations associated with regular investments and defined-contribution pension plans. This means that your Social Security benefits are essentially guaranteed and are not subject to the threats of investment risks or financial market fluctuations. This is because your Social Security benefits are paid out of Social Security Trust Fund and backed by the full faith and credit of the United States government.

Social Security benefits are not means-tested and thus do not depend on your needs. In other words,

Social Security does not reduce or deny benefits to people whose income or assets exceed a certain level. This feature makes Social Security almost a universal program. The broad inclusiveness of Social Security is why nearly all American workers participate in Social Security by making payroll tax contributions, and nearly 97 percent of all elderly Americans (ages 60–90 years) will receive some form of Social Security benefit.

Social Security provides a foundation of retirement protection for people at all earnings levels. Social Security was not intended to be the sole source of retirement income, rather, it fosters private pensions and personal saving because it is not based on need. It is also noteworthy that Social Security provides a higher annual payout than private retirement annuities per dollar contributed because its risk pool is broader and its administrative costs are relatively lower.

The average Social Security retirement benefit in 2019 was about $17,000 a year. Social Security benefits have been important for children and their families as well as for the elderly. Approximately 6 million children under age 18 lived in families that received income from Social Security in 2019, and nearly 2 million children were lifted out of poverty last year.

The average retiree gets about $1,400 per month ($17,000 per year) from Social Security. The maximum Social Security benefit a 65-year-old retiring in 2020 can get is $2,857 per month. The absolute maximum a new 70-year-old retiree can get in 2020 is $3,790 per month.

A recent study showed that over a third of elderly Americans would be poor without Social Security, and that the program lifts more than 10 million elderly Americans out of poverty. Note that Social Security provides the majority of income to most elderly Americans. For about half of elderly Americans, it provides at least 50 percent of their income, and for about one fifth of elderly Americans, it provides at least 90 percent of income.

Now, you can see why the broad scope of Social Security impacts nearly every American. And everyone should factor Social Security benefits into their retirement financial plans and independence. This book gives you a comprehensive but easy-to-understand explanation of the benefits you may be entitled to under Social Security, as well as tips to optimize benefits over your lifetime.

An important factor to enjoying your retirement will be your financial security. However, financial security does not just happen. It requires planning, commitment, and money. Although Social Security provides some good basic benefits, your financial independence in your retirement years will likely come from your pension, savings, investments, and other private financial resources. For an independent and fulfilling life you will need to set financial goals and work to achieve them. Make sure that you are thoroughly knowledgeable about your Social Security benefits, pensions, and other sources of financial support for your retirement.

CHAPTER 1

MAINTAINING YOUR INDEPENDENCE DURING RETIREMENT

Everyone wants an independent lifestyle after he or she retires. You want the financial, scheduling, health and emotional freedom to enjoy retirement years that are fulfilling and rewarding. After all, you have worked hard all your life, put in the long hours and travelled on business during many holidays. Without question, retirement is the only time in your adult life when you are free from the pressures of work and can truly be independent.

Keep in mind at all times that the basis for a happy and independent retirement is a life lived to the fullest. Your retirement years should be ones of peace and comfort spent in close, endearing relationships with family and friends. They should be a time for engaging in rewarding and satisfying activities and endeavors, and a time for travel, adventure, self-development, and personal enrichment.

But independence during retirement requires preparation long before you retire. As early as possible during your work life you should consider your retirement needs and take the steps to attain them. Taking control of your money, credit, insurance, health, and other resources is fundamental to your independence and overall well-being. The most important step in attaining independence is getting started. For many people, the problem is simply procrastination. People simply do not plan until a major situation has developed. This type of crisis planning is the least effective and is unlikely to lead to personal independence.

At least ten years before you plan to retire, preferably much sooner, you should sit down and determine your retirement needs. An independent retirement can be expensive, and financial experts estimate that you will need about 70 to 80 percent of your preretirement income to maintain your standard of living during retirement. For the average retiree, Social Security will pay only about 40 percent of preretirement earnings. If your present financial situation will not provide an adequate level of retirement income, you will need to make adjustments in your savings, spending, or income to make up for any deficiencies.

It is up to you to make your retirement dreams come true by setting and attaining financial goals. You should review your financial status on a regular basis by determining your net worth and analyzing how your assets are allocated. You should prepare a budget to keep track of your cash inflows and outflows. Set adequate and achievable goals for savings and investments to provide necessary resources for retirement. You should also do some estate planning to minimize taxes and administrative expenses, and to maximize value for your family, heirs, and other beneficiaries.

One view is that financial independence occurs when you have saved enough to support your current spending habits for the rest of your life without the need to earn more money. You might choose to work for other reasons, such as passion or purpose, but you no longer need a job to fund your lifestyle. You need to decide on your financial priorities for your retirement. Is it important that you have money to travel the world? Buy a sailboat? Leave a large inheritance for your heirs? Whatever your priorities, make sure that you will receive the optimum benefits from your pension, investments, Social Security, and other sources. Again, put your financial goals on paper and review them regularly to make sure that you are achieving your objectives.

You should maintain close contact with family and friends during retirement, and come to rely on them for help when you need it. Do not feel any guilt asking for help. At the same time, be willing to assist others when you can. Remember that family and friends cannot always be there for you because of any number of reasons. They may be far away, traveling constantly, overworked or facing other demands in their lives. This means that you must be realistic in your expectations of others in planning your retirement.

And now because we are living longer, healthier lives, we can expect to spend more time in retirement than our parents and grandparents did. Financial independence typically means having enough income to pay your living expenses for the rest of your life without having to work full time. Some people achieve this through investing and saving during their work life. Other people create successful businesses that can generate income without their daily supervision. There are many ways for you to reach financial independence, and it is not just for the wealthy.

SETTING FINANCIAL GOALS

Setting goals and objectives is critical for any effective financial plan. Start by listing and prioritizing realistic financial goals to create a working agenda. These goals should be revised periodically as conditions, needs, and other developments occur.

Some common financial goals are:

- reducing personal debt;
- providing adequate retirement income; and
- attaining financial security and independence.

Reducing Personal Debt:

Debt consolidation and reduction is perhaps one of the most important financial goals. With the elimination of the tax deductibility of consumer debt, credit card and other personal debt becomes a substantial drain on a person's cash. Many people get trapped in the spiral of just paying off interest and not the principal balances of these accounts. This allows the interest and principle to continue the compounding process. Although savings and certificate of deposit rates have fallen tremendously, the major credit cards are still charging in excess of 15 to 18 percent interest. These high consumer interest rates can spell disaster for financial planning and security.

You need to look at ways to control your personal debt by minimizing use of credit cards and consumer credit. Get rid of high interest debts and free your money to work for you instead of the banks. You should try to pay cash for most of your purchases if possible. You should avoid impulse buying as it can wreck your financial planning. Is too much being spent on gifts? Entertainment and dining out? Vacations? Clothing? One of the many reasons people spend so much money on stuff is to keep up with their friends and neighbors. Ignore the neighbors to build up your finances instead, and you will leave your neighbors behind financially. Although you should enjoy life, finding ways to curb your spending can help you in saving, investing, and meeting your financial goals.

Learning to use the equity in your home can help you manage your credit and advance your financial plans. Unlike consumer interest, part of your home mortgage and home equity are tax deductible. Consider getting a home equity loan to pay off consumer loans and consolidate debt. It will likely save taxes and interest in the long run. Various options are available for handling your real estate for maximum benefit, such as reverse mortgages, gifting and others.

Providing Adequate Retirement Income:
Although Social Security provides some basic benefits, your financial independence during retirement will likely come from your pensions, savings, investments, and other financial resources. This means that now more than ever you will be responsible for providing for your own retirement.

As mentioned earlier, during retirement you will need approximately 70 to 80 percent of your preretirement income to maintain your standard of living. A major portion of your retirement income will likely be the result of your personal savings and investments. Do not forget the importance of your employer-sponsored 401(k) plan in saving for your retirement, and use your 401(k) to maximize your financial benefits. You should try to contribute as much as possible to your 401(k) plan. The earnings that you save are usually tax-deferred, and many employers match the

401(k) contributions. Also, you can typically borrow money from your 401(k) at below market rates and the interest is tax-deferred income to you. You can advantageously use your 401(k) loans to pay off credit and other consumer debts.

You can use the retirement planning Chart 1 below to set financial goals for retirement:

CHART 1: RETIREMENT PLANNING
Your Financial Needs

1. Annual income needed when you retire (80% of pre-retirement income).	$_____
2. Probable annual Social Security benefits.	$_____
3. Estimated annual pension.	$_____
4. Annual retirement income needed from investments (line 1 minus lines 2 and 3).	$_____
5. Amount you must save before retirement (line 4 times Factor A from Chart 3 below).	$_____
6. Amount you have saved already (including IRAs, corporate savings plans, and other investments).	$_____

Your Financial Needs

7. Projected value of your current retirement savings at the time you retire (line 6 times Factor B from Chart 4 below).	$_____
8. Amount of retirement funds still needed (line 5 minus line 7).	$_____
9. Annual savings needed to reach your goal (line 8 times Factor C from Chart 5 below).	$_____
10. Total amount you should save (line 9 minus any employer contributions to savings plan).	$_____

The figures in Chart 2 are for an individual who turns 62 in year 2020 and are in 2020 dollars (to include spousal benefits multiply the figures times 1.5). For example, if you turn 62 in year 2020 and have earned an average of $100,000 and you wait until you are 70 to claim benefits, you will receive about $41,800 per year plus any cost-of-living adjustments that are given over the next eight years. Although not shown in Chart 2, the maximum Social Security retirement benefit a 65-year-old retiring in 2020 will receive is $34,284 per year, and the maximum Social Security retirement benefit a 70-year-old retiring in 2020 will receive is $45,480 per year. The average retiree in 2020 will receive about $17,200 per year in Social Security retirement benefits.

CHART 2: ESTIMATED ANNUAL SOCIAL SECURITY BENEFIT PAYMENT BASED ON RETIREMENT AGE AND EARNINGS FOR YEAR 2020

Average Annual Earnings	Retirement Age				
	Age 62	Age 65	66 Years & 4 Months	Age 68	Age 70
$20,000	$9,200	$11,500	$12,600	$14,300	$16,400
$30,000	$11,600	$14,500	$15,900	$18,000	$20,500
$40,000	$14,000	$17,400	$19,100	$21,600	$24,700
$50,000	$16,300	$20,300	$22,300	$25,300	$28,800
$60,000	$18,700	$23,200	$25,500	$28,900	$33,000
$70,000	$20,400	$25,300	$27,800	$31,500	$36,000
$80,000	$21,500	$26,700	$29,300	$33,200	$37,900
$90,000	$22,600	$28,000	$30,800	$34,900	$39,800
$100,000	$23,700	$29,400	$32,300	$36,600	$41,800

Data Source: Author's Calculations

CHART 3

Age at Retirement	Factor A
55	23.3
56	22.9
57	22.6
58	22.2
59	21.8
60	21.4
61	21.0
62	20.5
63	20.1
64	19.6
65	19.2
66	18.7
67	18.2

It is difficult to calculate precisely how much your Social Security benefit payment will be if you are younger than age 62 because of variability in future earnings and inflation. But Chart 2 can give you a good estimate of your Social Security benefits in 2020 dollars. You can also get a good estimate of your Social Security benefit from your annual Social Security statement.

Attaining Financial Security and Independence:
What does financial independence really mean? The definition of financial security will be different

CHART 4

Years from Retirement	Factor B	Factor C
5	1.15	0.188
7	1.22	0.131
9	1.29	0.099
11	1.36	0.079
13	1.44	0.065
15	1.53	0.054
20	1.76	0.038
25	2.02	0.028
30	2.33	0.022

(The Factors listed above assume a hypothetical 8 percent total return and a 5 percent rate of inflation.)
Source: Social Security Administration

for each person. Your goal of financial security may be creating a portfolio of $1 million in marketable securities which will allow you to live off the interest and dividends. It may be having a pension and Social Security benefits of $100,000 a year. Or it may be having one or two years earnings saved to protect you in case of unemployment or an emergency.

With financial independence there is no one size fits all because everyone has different lifestyles and standards of living. Some advisers take the position that there are various levels of financial security and independence. Some feel that financial independence is not all about having sufficient funds to cover all of your expenses and customary lifestyle. Financial independence could as well mean the ability to conquer your psychological fears and worries about money and live a free and full life. Retirement itself can be viewed as attaining financial independence in the third stage of life.

Whatever your idea of financial security and independence is, a good financial planner can be helpful in analyzing your finances and recommending how to improve your financial situation. He or she can assist in preparing a financial plan based on your personal history and financial goals. However, before selecting a financial planner, be sure to investigate his or her background and experience.

A successful strategy for optimizing your financial security should comprise 1) controlling your personal debts and expenditures, 2) saving regularly, 3) taking full advantage of tax-deferred and tax-free income plans, and 4) maintaining a diversified and risk-balanced investment portfolio.

Your investment strategy should be one of prudent risk-taking. With most investments, the greater risks usually provide the potential for a greater return to you. However, your level of risk-taking typically changes over the various cycles of your life. At a younger age you can afford to take greater risks as you strive to build up your investment assets. When you approach retirement, your risk factor should decline as you focus on minimizing losses and preserving asset value. To help you reduce overall risk of loss, your investment portfolio should always be diversified into a variety of investment vehicles.

CASH FLOW MANAGEMENT

Managing your disposable income is critical in allowing you to reach your financial security goals and objectives. A starting point is to establish a workable budget using the cash flow worksheet Chart 5 on page 20.

Preparing a budget helps you keep track of where your money is going. It also helps to predict how you will likely spend money in the future. Budgeting is an important process in setting financial goals and making sure that you are taking the right steps toward meeting them. Start by listing all your sources of monthly income such as salary and wages, pensions, annuities, Social Security payments, interest, dividends, rental income, gifts, and any other money that you receive. Then itemize all of your monthly expenditures and expenses including mortgage, rent, taxes, utilities, insurance, repairs, loans and credit card payments, food, clothing, transportation, recreation and the like. A helpful exercise is to make journal entries on all cash expenditures on a daily or weekly basis.

Once all of the major expense categories have been identified, it is important to establish spending

CHART 5

Cash Flow Worksheet		Per Month
Income:	Wages, salary and commissions	$_____
	Dividends, interest and realized capital gains	$_____
	Annuities	$_____
	Pensions	$_____
	IRAs and 401(k) distributions	$_____
	Payments from trusts and estates	$_____
	Rental or other income from real estate	$_____
	Other	$_____
	Total Income	$_____
Expenses:	Mortgage/Rent	$_____
	Utilities	$_____
	Telephone	$_____
	Medical Expenses	$_____
	Car/Transportation	$_____
	Food	$_____
	Clothing	$_____
	Childcare	$_____

Insurance premiums $_____

Home repairs $_____

Loans and credit card $_____
payments

Tuition/education $_____
expenses

Hobbies $_____

Entertainment $_____

Vacations $_____

Other $_____

Total Expenses $_____

Total Income: $_____ minus
Total Expenses: $_____
equals
Total available for savings/investments:
$_____

guidelines for all areas. Subtracting your total expenses from your total income gives you the disposable income to use for savings and investments. Ideally, your income should be more than your expenses and spending, especially during your preretirement years to allow for savings.

DETERMINING YOUR NET WORTH

Determining your net worth periodically lets you know where you are financially. Your net worth is calculated by totaling all of your assets and subtracting all of your debts and other liabilities. You can start with the preparation of a net worth statement by listing all of your assets and their value. This should include cash, checking and savings accounts, certificates of deposit, stocks, bonds, IRAs, 401(k)s, life insurance cash value, real estate, automobiles, and all of your personal property. Next, you list all of your liabilities including mortgages, personal loans, credit card balances, taxes, and any other debts. The sum of your assets minus your total liabilities will tell you how much you are worth monetarily.

Use the net worth statement Chart 6 on page 23 to calculate your net worth.

YOUR INVESTMENT OPTIONS

There are a myriad of savings and investment vehicles available for both short-term and long financial goals. These include everything from the simple savings accounts with banks, credit unions, and savings and loan associations to US government securities, corporate and municipal bonds, mutual funds, annuities, stock, real estate and commodities. An effective investment strategy is to balance risks, yields, taxes, inflation and liquidity with the best mix of investment channels.

Financial planners have various investing guidelines depending on your age and investment horizons. One example is: subtract your age from one

CHART 6
Net Worth Statement
Assets (Current Value)

Liquid Assets:
Cash	$_____
Checking accounts	_____
Savings accounts	_____
Money market funds	_____
Cash value of life insurance	_____
Other liquid assets	_____
Total Liquid Assets	_____

Investment Assets:
Stocks	$_____
Bonds	_____
Mutual funds	_____
Certificates of deposit	_____
Other investment assets	_____
Total Investment Assets	_____

Retirement Plans:
IRAs	$_____
401(k)s	_____
Annuities	_____
Vested pension value	_____
Other retirement plans	_____

Total Retirement Plan Assets _____

Personal Assets:

Real Estate $_____

Automobiles   _____

Jewelry/art/antiques   _____

Other personal assets   _____

Total Personal Assets   _____

Total Assets $_____

Liabilities

Mortgage $_____

Credit card balances   _____

Auto mobile loans   _____

Education loans   _____

Personal loans   _____

Taxes   _____

Other debts and liabilities   _____

Total Liabilities $_____

Total Assets $_____ minus

Total Liabilities $_____ equals

Your Net Worth $_____

hundred. That number represents the percentage of your assets that should be in stocks. Always remember that your investment portfolio should always be diversified into a variety of investment vehicles.

The US Government offers securities which are very safe with guaranteed rates of return (although lower than commercial securities). Treasury bills are short-term securities with maturities ranging from a few days to a year, and they are redeemable for face value. You pay a discounted price, and the yield over the time period is the difference between the face value and the discounted price. You can purchase Treasury bills directly from your local federal reserve bank without paying any fees or through an intermediary bank or broker.

The US Treasury also offers Treasury notes which are issued with maturities of 2, 3, 5, 7, and 10 years and pay interest every six months. Treasury bonds have a maturity of 30 years and pay interest every six months. Treasury notes and bonds are very safe investments and can usually be purchased through banks and other financial institutions, or your employer by payroll deduction.

Municipal bonds are another relatively safe investment vehicle. Although their yields are usually lower than riskier investments, the interest earned is typically exempt from federal, state, and local taxes. Municipal bonds can be a useful investment medium if you are in a high tax bracket.

Corporate bonds are an additional investment option which can offer attractive yields at relatively low to medium risks, depending on the financial health of the issuing company and its bond rating.

Bonds with the highest grade are rated a "AAA" and these typically offer a lower yield than the lower-grade bonds. Corporate bonds are usually issued from one to thirty years and are redeemable for the face value at maturity. You purchase the bonds at a discounted price that fluctuates according to market conditions.

You are probably already familiar with the savings plans offered by your bank, such as the traditional savings account. Banks also offer certificates of deposit with varying maturity periods and interest rates. There are usually penalties for early withdrawal of funds from certificates of deposit. Money market accounts are also available at most banks and generally earn a higher yield than your regular bank savings account. The money market accounts may provide check writing and other privileges, and may be subject to minimum balance requirements and administrative fees. Your accounts with federally insured banks and credit unions are insured up to $250,000 per depositor.

Annuities from insurance companies or other financial establishments are investment vehicles which guarantee a fixed income for life or a specified number of years. If you want a guaranteed income without having to worry about managing your asset to attain it, then you may want to think about purchasing an annuity. The earnings are usually tax-deferred until you make withdrawals. Annuities are only as good as the company issuing them, so be sure to investigate the financial health of the company before purchasing an annuity.

Riskier investments include equity or ownership interests such as stocks, mutual funds, commodities and real estate. When you purchase stock, you are buying part ownership in a company. The value of your stock will go up and down depending on the financial performance of the company and other economic conditions. The stock may also pay dividends determined by company profits. Regular ownership in a company is evidenced by common stock which has no guaranteed rate of return; in fact, the return can be negative if the stock price falls. Preferred stock usually offers a specified dividend rate and is paid off before common stock if the company dissolves. Historically, stocks have outperformed most other financial assets such as bonds, money markets, and metals. Over a twenty-year horizon a stock portfolio, on average, will likely generate the most growth and help keep assets above inflation.

Mutual funds are a mechanism for you to pool your assets with other investors for investing in a variety of vehicles. Some mutual funds can be speculative and extremely risky and others can be conservative depending on how the fund is managed and makes investments. It is very important that you evaluate a fund's historical performance and financial stability before investing in mutual funds.

Real estate and commodities are highly speculative investments and involve a lot of risk. With these investments you are betting on the future value of assets such as real property, precious metals, feed stocks, and foreign currencies. Always obtain professional advice before investing in high-risk ventures.

Here are some wealth generating habits that will help to make financial security and independence a part of your future:

- Coordinate and optimize the major elements of your retirement portfolio—your benefits from pensions, savings and investments, and Social Security benefits.
- Make sure that you are spending notably less than you earn by budgeting and exploring new sources of income.
- Prioritize savings ahead of everything else by paying yourself first, before you pay other bills, so you learn to live on a contained budget (living with what is left after paying yourself is a great way to build wealth).
- Invest your money in assets that will generate income (such as interest, dividends, rentals, etc.) and appreciate in value.

- Never stop saving and investing over the long term; even during good and bad years, but adjust your asset allocation near retirement to reduce risk and volatility.
- Be adaptable to conserve savings and adjust spending and income during financially difficult times; such as getting a part-time job instead of withdrawing from savings.

DETERMINING YOUR LIVING ARRANGEMENTS

A major decision affecting retirement is where to live. Staying independent and living at home is generally the preferred living arrangement for most retirees. However, physical, medical, or financial problems can often prevent this from happening. Do you sell your home? Move to a better climate? Relocate close to family? Be sure to analyze the living costs, access to medical care, and the tax consequences of any move that you plan to make during retirement.

Before you move, do your research on the new location. Will it provide the various social services and recreational and cultural activities that you might need during retirement? Check on the availability of good medical care, neighborhood safety, transportation, and other features that are important to you. Consider renting for some time before buying a home to make sure you are comfortable with the new surroundings.

Whether you are moving across town or across the country, there are a number of housing options for retirement. These include retirement communities, assisted living housing, life-care centers, condominiums, apartments, and single-family homes. Many of these options offer savings on housing expenses, freedom from care-taking, opportunities to interact with peers, and a variety of health care and social services. Consider all of the housing alternatives and decide on the one which provides the greatest benefits and enjoyment for your retirement.

Retirement communities provide social benefits because they are populated by people of retirement age. These communities typically limit residents to senior citizens and may have restrictions on guests or pets. Usually there are several types of housing and a wide range of services and activities are available. These can include transportation, recreation, financial services, medical care, security, group dining, and social events. The retirement community lifestyle may appear too structured for many people, but it remains attractive for many retirees.

Assisted-living housing can be a useful arrangement if health considerations or physical limitations prevent you from living alone or performing certain daily activities. This arrangement usually provides private living quarters in an apartment-style setting with support services for physical activities or medical care from staff or other residents. Life-care centers may be a housing option for retirees who require custodial care or constant medical attention. You typically pay an admission fee and/or a monthly service fee and are guaranteed housing for life.

Condominiums are a popular housing choice for many retirees because they offer a comfortable and convenient living arrangement without the responsibilities of maintenance and upkeep. These apartment-style homes are purchased instead of rented and common areas such as atriums, courtyards, and hallways are shared with other residents. A monthly fee is charged for maintenance and other services by the condominium association.

As you get older, you may have to make a decision between independent living and assisted living. The biggest difference between these two options is the amount of care that you will need. Independent living can mean staying in your home, but it typically is associated with residential living in a senior citizen community. Some retirees move to an independent living facility for financial reasons because they do not want to continue maintaining a big house. Others may choose independent living for social reasons and want to surround themselves with other people in the same stage of life.

Independent living communities are commonly in the form of an apartment building or condominium complex. Depending on the facility, residents can either rent or buy. These residences typically provide full-home independence and can be purchased or rented by the residents. Typically independent living facilities come with many ease-of-living services, such as housekeeping and laundry services, dining rooms with prepared meals, and maintenance and grounds keeping.

Assisted living is generally for people who need assistance with their day-to-day life. A typical assisted-living home will have residences that range from full apartments to individual rooms in a facility set up similar to an apartment building. Residents in assisted living usually have access to common spaces and a dining room that serves prepared meals, but they often live much of their lives independently from the broader community. The assisted-living facility will provide some nursing or other service staff for the residents, but will not provide comprehensive medical care like a nursing home.

Financial independence and security also requires that you be prepared for a medical emergency. What is your plan if you were to suddenly become sick and unable to communicate or care for yourself. Decide on someone you trust that you would want to make necessary medical decisions for you and set up a health-care directive. Additionally, decide if you would benefit from wearing a medical alert device.

Many retirees would prefer to age in place at their home rather than change their living arrangement. But you have to plan ahead to age in place and think about the kinds of help you might need in the near future. Evaluate any illnesses or health issues that you or your spouse might have which could make it difficult for you to get around or take care of yourself in the future, and make a plan to handle these situations. Your family, friends, and neighbors can be a major source of help for you.

FINDING JOY AND INNER PEACE

A major key to happiness is finding joy and inner peace despite the stress and worries of everyday life. You need some stress in your life because it brings challenges and opportunities or life would be dull and unexciting. But, too much stress can seriously affect your physical and mental health. Your goal in this stress-filled world is to find a way to manage the stress in your life and make it work for you instead of against you.

Although work-related stress may not exist during retirement, stress will still come from physical, mental, and emotional activities that you undertake every day. Stress is so personal that things that may be relaxing to others may be stressful for you. For instance, you may be the type of person who likes being busy and active most of the time. A day of "taking it easy" or "doing nothing" at the beach may make you feel unproductive and frustrated. Yet others may find such days quite relaxing. Find out what you like and relax your way. Oftentimes, too much stress is caused by trying to conform to other people's expectations.

Too much emotional stress can lead to physical illnesses, such as high blood pressure, ulcers, and heart disease. It can also lead to depression, mental illness, and even suicide. Recognizing the early signs of overstress, and doing something about them, can make a big difference in the quality of your life.

You can relieve some stress in your life through exercise or physical activity. Biking, walking, playing golf, or gardening are just some of the activities you might try. It also helps to talk to someone about your concerns and worries. Perhaps a friend, family member, or counselor can help you see your problem in a different light. If you feel that your problem is serious enough, you might seek professional help from a psychologist, psychiatrist, social worker, or mental health counselor. Knowing when to ask for help may avoid more serious problems later.

Getting enough rest and eating well will also help you deal with stress. If you are irritable and tense from lack of sleep, or if you are not eating correctly, you will have less ability to deal with stressful situations. If stress repeatedly keeps you from sleeping, you should ask your doctor for help. Although you can use prescription or over-the-counter medications to relieve stress temporarily, these do not remove the conditions that caused the stress in the first place. Medications, in fact, may be habit-forming and reduce your ability to function, thus creating more stress than they take away. They should be taken only on the advice of your doctor.

The best strategy for avoiding stress is to learn how to relax. Unfortunately, many people try to relax at the same pace that they lead the rest of their lives. For a while, tune out your worries about time, productivity, and "doing right." You will find satisfaction in just being, without striving. Find activities that give you pleasure and that are good for your mental and physical well-being. Forget about always winning. Focus on relaxation, enjoyment, and health.

One way to keep from getting bored, sad, or lonely during retirement is to go where things are happening. Sitting alone can make you feel disheartened. Instead of feeling sorry for yourself, get involved and become a participant. Offer your services to neighborhood or volunteer organizations. Help yourself by helping other people. Get involved in the world and the people around you, and you will find they will be attracted to you. You will be on your way to making new friends and enjoying new activities.

Travel is a very popular and rewarding leisure activity among retirees. Whether in the United States or abroad, traveling can be an experience that brings enrichment, fulfillment, and a sense of independence. Whatever your budget, you can and should make travel a part of your retirement plan.

Millions of retired Americans participate in continuing adult education at community colleges, universities and other forums. This is an excellent avenue for personal development and socialization. A network of several hundred colleges, schools and other institutions, called "Road Scholar" (formerly "Elderhostel"), offer low-cost, short-term, residential and travel academic programs for older adults. Adult education programs are also sponsored by local public school systems. Investigate these programs to see how they can give some benefit and fulfillment to you. Take advantage of museums and libraries. These institutions provide opportunities for learning, enrichment, and leisure-time activities.

CHAPTER 2

THE IMPORTANCE OF SOCIAL SECURITY

Social Security Provides a Family Safety Net

As mentioned earlier, Social Security is very important because it delivers an important financial safety net for American families. Social Security can be an essential factor in your financial and personal independence. It reaches almost every family and eventually touches the lives of nearly all Americans. Social Security helps senior citizens, disabled workers, and families where a spouse or parent has died. In 2019, over 175 million people worked and paid Social Security taxes and over 60 million people received monthly Social Security benefits. About 46 million Social Security beneficiaries were retirees and their families in 2019.

Keep in mind that Social Security was never meant to be the only source of income for people when they retire. Social Security only replaces a percentage of a worker's preretirement income based on his or her lifetime earnings. The amount of your average wages that Social Security retirement benefits replaces varies depending on your earnings and when you choose to start benefits. If you start benefits at full retirement age, this percentage equates to as much as 75 percent for very low earners, to about 40 percent for medium earners, and to about 27 percent for high earners. These benefits are higher if you start benefits after your full retirement age, and these percentages are lower if you start your benefits earlier. The common projection from most financial advisers is that you will need about 70 percent of preretirement income to live comfortably in retirement, including your Social Security benefits, private pensions, personal savings and investments. Thus, it is extremely important that you understand how you and your family's financial future will be impacted by Social Security.

Basically, you will qualify for Social Security by working and paying Social Security taxes to earn Social Security credits. You earned one credit for each $1,410 of earnings in 2020 up to a maximum of four credits per year. Usually, the amount of earnings required to earn a Social Security credit increases each year. Generally, you need at least 40 credits (equivalent to 10 years of work) to qualify for Social Security retirement benefits. You will need less Social Security for you to qualify for disability benefits or for your family members to be eligible for survivors' benefits when you die. Make the Social Security safety net work for you and your family by analyzing and maximizing these benefits.

SUMMARY OF SOCIAL SECURITY BENEFITS AND BENEFICIARIES

Basically, the Social Security program provides three kinds of important benefits. They include retirement, disability, and survivors benefits. This book will discuss each of these benefits and provide information to help you and your family optimize the benefits that you are entitled to.

Do not forget that if you qualify for retirement or disability benefits, then others in your family might also qualify to receive benefits. For example, your spouse is eligible if he or she is at least 62 years old. Your spouse is also eligible, based on your Social Security record, if under age 62 and caring for your child who is i) under age 16, or ii) age 16 and older (but disabled). Your unmarried children are also eligible to receive benefits because of your record if they are i) under age 18, ii) age 18–19 and attending elementary or high school full-time, or iii) 18 or older with a disability. Further, if you are divorced, your ex-spouse could be eligible for benefits on your Social Security record.

Here is a comprehensive list of people who can receive benefits under Social Security:

- people who have already retired;
- people who are disabled;
- survivors of workers who have died;
- dependents of beneficiaries;
- a spouse or child of someone getting benefits;
- a divorced spouse of someone getting or eligible for Social Security;
- a spouse or child of a worker who died;
- a divorced spouse of a worker who died; and
- a dependent parent of a worker who died.

Each of these Social Security recipients will be further discussed in later chapters of this book.

Depending on your circumstances, you may be eligible to receive Social Security benefits at any age.

If you have worked long enough, Social Security will pay you your full retirement benefits when you reach full retirement age or will pay reduced benefits as early as age 62. Your Social Security retirement benefits are based on how much you earned during your working career. Higher lifetime earnings result in higher benefits. If there were some years when you did no work, or had low earnings, your benefit amount may be lower than if you had a steady work history.

Although Social Security Administration keeps a record of your earnings and provides an estimate of your Social Security retirement benefits, the taxes that you pay into Social Security are not held in a dedicated personal account for you. Instead, the Social Security taxes are used to pay people who are currently receiving benefits, and any Social Security taxes which are not used are held in the general Social Security trust funds.

CHAPTER 3

YOUR SOCIAL SECURITY NUMBER

Your Social Security number is your main identifier and link to Social Security Administration. The Social Security Administration utilizes your Social Security number to keep track of your earnings record during your work life and to determine your Social Security benefits when you are receiving them. Your Social Security number is also necessary in obtaining a job, getting a loan or other credit, opening a bank account, and paying taxes.

Social Security Administration will keep your Social Security number and your records in confidence. Social Security Administration will not give someone else any information about you or your account, unless you have given your written consent or unless required or permitted by law.

You should always safeguard your Social Security number and be very careful about giving your Social

Security number to someone to avoid fraud and identity theft. You should not carry your Social Security card on you, but keep it in a safe and secure place. An identity thief can use your Social Security number and your good credit record to obtain credit cards, loans, and other lines of credit in your name.

You should contact or visit Social Security Administration directly if you need a Social Security number or if you lost your Social Security card and need a replacement card. Also, contact Social Security Administration if you need to change your name on your Social Security card. You will need to complete a simple application and provide certain documents. Social Security Administration will generally require documents which are originals or copies certified by the issuing office. Photocopies of documents or notarized copies will not be acceptable to Social Security Administration.

For you to get a Social Security number or a replacement Social Security card, you will have to prove your identity, age, US citizenship, or (if you are not a US citizen) immigration status, age, and identity. You do not have to show proof of your US citizenship and age for a replacement card if that information is already in your Social Security records.

Social Security Administration will only accept certain documents as proof of your US citizenship. The acceptable documents include your US birth certificate, US passport, Certificate of Naturalization, or Certificate of Citizenship. For non-US citizens, Social Security Administration will require your immigration document proving work authorization. Different rules will apply if you do not have authorization to work in the United States.

To prove your identity, Social Security Administration will accept current documents showing your name, identifying information and preferably a recent photograph, such as a driver's license or other state-issued identification card, or a US passport.

If you want to apply for a change of name on your Social Security card, you must show a recently issued document that proves your name has been legally changed.

Be sure to keep your Social Security card in a safe and secure place. This will help to prevent fraud and identity theft. And Social Security Administration will typically limit you to no more than i) 3 replacement cards in a year and ii) 10 replacement cards during your lifetime. Some exceptions may not apply if you have a legal name change, a change in your citizenship status, or if you can prove that the replacement card is needed to prevent a significant hardship. All of the Social Security Administration card services are free.

For more information about your Social Security card, read "Your Social Security Number and Card" (Publication No. 05–10002). If you are not a citizen, read "Social Security Numbers for Noncitizens" (Publication No. 05–10096).

An Application for a Social Security Card (Form SS-5) and instructions are provided below and can be found online at www.ssa.gov/forms/.

One of the things that you should do when you have a baby is to get a Social Security number for your child. The easiest time to do this is at the hospital when you give information for your child's birth certificate. If you wait until later and apply for a number at a Social Security office, they will have to verify the child's birth certificate which can cause delays.

There are several good reasons why you should get a Social Security number for your child. You may need a Social Security number to:

- claim your child as a dependent on your income tax return;
- open a bank account for your child;
- buy savings bonds for your child;
- get medical coverage for your child; or
- apply for government services for your child.

So, getting a Social Security number when your child is born is a good idea, but it is not mandatory that you get a number for your new baby.

You can apply for your new child's Social Security number at the hospital or at a Social Security Office.

When you give information for your baby's birth certificate at the hospital, you will be asked whether you want to apply for a Social Security number for your baby. If you say "yes," you will be requested to provide both parents' Social Security numbers if you can. But, you can still apply for a Social Security number for your child even if you do not know both parents' Social Security numbers. If you apply at a Social Security office you are required to complete an application for a Social Security card and show original documents proving your child's US citizenship, age, and identity. You must also provide documents which prove your identity and your relationship to the child. Any child age 12 or older who requests an original Social Security number must appear in person for an interview, even if a parent or guardian will sign the application on the child's behalf.

Social Security Administration will only accept certain documents as proof of US citizenship. These include a US birth certificate, US consular report of birth, US passport, Certificate of Naturalization or Certificate of Citizenship.

(Information in the following form and instructions is taken from publications and other sources from the US Social Security Administration. This information is not intended as an endorsement or recommendation of this book, the author, or the publisher by US Social Security or any governmental agency.)

Form **SS-5** (11-2019) UF
Discontinue Prior Editions
SOCIAL SECURITY ADMINISTRATION

Page 1 of 5

OMB No. 0960-0066

Application for a Social Security Card

Applying for a Social Security Card is free!

USE THIS APPLICATION TO:

- Apply for an original Social Security card
- Apply for a replacement Social Security card
- Change or correct information on your Social Security number record

IMPORTANT: You MUST provide a properly completed application and the required evidence before we can process your application. We can only accept original documents or documents certified by the custodian of the original record. Notarized copies or photocopies which have not been certified by the custodian of the record are not acceptable. We will return any documents submitted with your application. For assistance call us at 1-800-772-1213 or visit our website at **www.socialsecurity.gov**.

Original Social Security Card

To apply for an original card, you must provide at least two documents to prove age, identity, and U.S. citizenship or current lawful, work-authorized immigration status. If you are not a U.S. citizen and do not have DHS work authorization, you must prove that you have a valid non-work reason for requesting a card. See page 2 for an explanation of acceptable documents.

NOTE: If you are age 12 or older and have never received a Social Security number, you must apply in person.

Replacement Social Security Card

To apply for a replacement card, you must provide one document to prove your identity. If you were born outside the U.S., you must also provide documents to prove your U.S. citizenship or current, lawful, work-authorized status. See page 2 for an explanation of acceptable documents.

Changing Information on Your Social Security Record

To change the information on your Social Security number record (i.e., a name or citizenship change, or corrected date of birth) you must provide documents to prove your identity, support the requested change, and establish the reason for the change. For example, you may provide a birth certificate to show your correct date of birth. A document supporting a name change must be recent and identify you by both your old and new names. If the name change event occurred over two years ago or if the name change document does not have enough information to prove your identity, you must also provide documents to prove your identity in your prior name and/or in some cases your new legal name. If you were born outside the U.S. you must provide a document to prove your U.S. citizenship or current lawful, work-authorized status. See page 2 for an explanation of acceptable documents.

LIMITS ON REPLACEMENT SOCIAL SECURITY CARDS

Public Law 108-458 limits the number of replacement Social Security cards you may receive to 3 per calendar year and 10 in a lifetime. Cards issued to reflect changes to your legal name or changes to a work authorization legend do not count toward these limits. We may also grant exceptions to these limits if you provide evidence from an official source to establish that a Social Security card is required.

IF YOU HAVE ANY QUESTIONS

If you have any questions about this form or about the evidence documents you must provide, please visit our website at www.socialsecurity.gov for additional information as well as locations of our offices and Social Security Card Centers. You may also call Social Security at 1-800-772-1213. You can also find your nearest office or Card Center in your local phone book.

EVIDENCE DOCUMENTS

The following lists are examples of the types of documents you must provide with your application and are not all inclusive. Call us at 1-800-772-1213 if you cannot provide these documents.

IMPORTANT : If you are completing this application on behalf of someone else, you must provide evidence that shows your authority to sign the application as well as documents to prove your identity and the identity of the person for whom you are filing the application. We can only accept original documents or documents certified by the custodian of the original record. Notarized copies or photocopies which have not been certified by the custodian of the record are not acceptable.

Evidence of Age
In general, you must provide your birth certificate. In some situations, we may accept another document that shows your age. Some of the other documents we may accept are:

- U.S. hospital record of your birth (created at the time of birth)
- Religious record established before age five showing your age or date of birth
- Passport
- Final Adoption Decree (the adoption decree must show that the birth information was taken from the original birth certificate)

Evidence of Identity
You must provide current, unexpired evidence of identity in your legal name. Your legal name will be shown on the Social Security card. Generally, we prefer to see documents issued in the U.S. Documents you submit to establish identity must show your legal name AND provide biographical information (your date of birth, age, or parents' names) **and/or** physical information (photograph, or physical description - height, eye and hair color, etc.). If you send a photo identity document but do not appear in person, the document must show your biographical information (e.g., your date of birth, age, or parents' names). Generally, documents without an expiration date should have been issued within the past two years for adults and within the past four years for children.

As proof of your identity, you must provide a:

- U.S. driver's license; or
- U.S. State-issued non-driver identity card; or
- U.S. passport

If you do not have one of the documents above or cannot get a replacement within 10 work days, we may accept other documents that show your legal name and biographical information, such as a U.S. military identity card, Certificate of Naturalization, employee identity card, certified copy of medical record (clinic, doctor or hospital), health insurance card, Medicaid card, or school identity card/record. For young children, we may accept medical records (clinic, doctor, or hospital) maintained by the medical provider. We may also accept a final adoption decree, or a school identity card, or other school record maintained by the school.

If you are not a U.S. citizen, we must see your current U.S. immigration document(s) and your foreign passport with biographical information or photograph.

WE CANNOT ACCEPT A BIRTH CERTIFICATE, HOSPITAL SOUVENIR BIRTH CERTIFICATE, SOCIAL SECURITY CARD STUB OR A SOCIAL SECURITY RECORD as evidence of identity.

Evidence of U.S. Citizenship
In general, you must provide your U.S. birth certificate or U.S. Passport. Other documents you may provide are a Consular Report of Birth, Certificate of Citizenship, or Certificate of Naturalization.

Evidence of Immigration Status
You must provide a current unexpired document issued to you by the Department of Homeland Security (DHS) showing your immigration status, such as Form I-551, I-94, or I-766. If you are an international student or exchange visitor, you may need to provide additional documents, such as Form I-20, DS-2019, or a letter authorizing employment from your school and employer (F-1) or sponsor (J-1). We CANNOT accept a receipt showing you applied for the document. If you are not authorized to work in the U.S., we can issue you a Social Security card only if you need the number for a valid non-work reason. Your card will be marked to show you cannot work and if you do work, we will notify DHS. See page 3, item 5 for more information.

Form SS-5 (11-2019) UF   Page 3 of 5

HOW TO COMPLETE THIS APPLICATION

Complete and sign this application LEGIBLY using ONLY black or blue ink on the attached or downloaded form using only 8 ½" x 11" (or A4 8.25" x 11.7") paper.

GENERAL: Items on the form are self-explanatory or are discussed below. The numbers match the numbered items on the form. If you are completing this form for someone else, please complete the items as they apply to that person.

4. Show the month, day, and full (4 digit) year of birth; for example, "1998" for year of birth.

5. If you check "Legal Alien Not Allowed to Work" or "Other," you must provide a document from a U.S. Federal, State, or local government agency that explains why you need a Social Security number and that you meet all the requirements for the government benefit. NOTE: Most agencies do not require that you have a Social Security number. Contact us to see if your reason qualifies for a Social Security number.

6., 7. Providing race and ethnicity information is voluntary and is requested for informational and statistical purposes only. Your choice whether to answer or not does not affect decisions we make on your application. If you do provide this information, we will treat it very carefully.

9.B., 10.B. If you are applying for an original Social Security card for a child under age 18, you MUST show the parents' Social Security numbers unless the parent was never assigned a Social Security number. If the number is not known and you cannot obtain it, check the "unknown" box.

13. If the date of birth you show in item 4 is different from the date of birth currently shown on your Social Security record, show the date of birth currently shown on your record in item 13 and provide evidence to support the date of birth shown in item 4.

16. Show an address where you can receive your card 7 to 14 days from now.

17. WHO CAN SIGN THE APPLICATION? If you are age 18 or older and are physically and mentally capable of reading and completing the application, you must sign in item 17. If you are under age 18, you may either sign yourself, or a parent or legal guardian may sign for you. If you are over age 18 and cannot sign on your own behalf, a legal guardian, parent, or close relative may generally sign for you. If you cannot sign your name, you should sign with an "X" mark and have two people sign as witnesses in the space beside the mark. Please do not alter your signature by including additional information on the signature line as this may invalidate your application. Call us if you have questions about who may sign your application.

HOW TO SUBMIT THIS APPLICATION

In most cases, you can take or mail this signed application with your documents to any Social Security office. Any documents you mail to us will be returned to you. Go to https://secure.ssa.gov/apps6z/FOLO/fo001.jsp to find the Social Security office or Social Security Card Center that serves your area.

Form **SS-5** (11-2019) UF   Page 4 of 5

PROTECT YOUR SOCIAL SECURITY NUMBER AND CARD

Protect your SSN card and number from loss and identity theft. DO NOT carry your SSN card with you. Keep it in a secure location and only take it with you when you must show the card; e.g., to obtain a new job, open a new bank account, or to obtain benefits from certain U.S. agencies. Use caution in giving out your Social Security number to others, particularly during phone, mail, email and Internet requests you did not initiate.

PRIVACY ACT STATEMENT
Collection and Use of Personal Information

Sections 205(c) and 702 of the Social Security Act, as amended, allow us to collect this information. Furnishing us this information is voluntary. However, failing to provide all or part of the information may prevent us from assigning you a Social Security number (SSN) and issuing you a new or replacement Social Security card.

We will use the information to assign you an SSN and issue you a new or replacement Social Security card. We may also share your information for the following purposes, called routine uses:

- To Federal, State, and local entities to assist them with administering income maintenance and health maintenance programs, when a Federal statute authorizes them to use the SSN; and,

- To the Department of State for administering the Social Security Act in foreign countries through its facilities and services.

In addition, we may share this information in accordance with the Privacy Act and other Federal laws. For example, where authorized, we may use and disclose this information in computer matching programs, in which our records are compared with other records to establish or verify a person's eligibility for Federal benefit programs and for repayment of incorrect or delinquent debts under these programs.

A list of additional routine uses is available in our Privacy Act System of Records Notice (SORN) 60-0058, entitled Master Files of Social Security Number (SSN) Holders and SSN Applications, as published in the Federal Register (FR) on December 29, 2010, at 75 FR 82121. Additional information, and a full listing of all of our SORNs, is available on our website at www.ssa.gov/privacy.

Paperwork Reduction Act Statement - This information collection meets the requirements of 44 U.S.C. § 3507, as amended by section 2 of the Paperwork Reduction Act of 1995. You do not need to answer these questions unless we display a valid Office of Management and Budget control number. We estimate that it will take about 8.5 to 9.5 minutes to read the instructions, gather the facts, and answer the questions. **SEND OR BRING THE COMPLETED FORM TO YOUR LOCAL SOCIAL SECURITY OFFICE. You can find your local Social Security office through SSA's website at www.socialsecurity.gov. Offices are also listed under U. S. Government agencies in your telephone directory or you may call Social Security at 1-800-772-1213 (TTY 1-800-325-0778).** *You may send comments on our time estimate above to: SSA, 6401 Security Blvd, Baltimore, MD 21235-6401. Send only comments relating to our time estimate to this address, not the completed form.*

Form **SS-5** (11-2019) UF
Discontinue Prior Editions
SOCIAL SECURITY ADMINISTRATION

Page 5 of 5
OMB No. 0960-0066

Application for a Social Security Card

		First	Full Middle Name	Last
1	**NAME** TO BE SHOWN ON CARD			
	FULL NAME AT BIRTH IF OTHER THAN ABOVE	First	Full Middle Name	Last
	OTHER NAMES USED			

2	Social Security number previously assigned to the person listed in item 1	☐☐☐ ☐☐ ☐☐☐☐

3	**PLACE OF BIRTH** (Do Not Abbreviate) City State or Foreign Country	Office Use Only FCI	**4**	**DATE OF BIRTH** MM/DD/YYYY

5	**CITIZENSHIP** (Check One)	☐ U.S. Citizen	☐ Legal Alien Allowed To Work	☐ Legal Alien **Not Allowed To** Work (See Instructions On Page 3)	☐ Other (See Instructions On Page 3)

6	**ETHNICITY** Are You Hispanic or Latino? (Your Response is Voluntary) ☐ Yes ☐ No	**7**	**RACE** Select One or More (Your Response is Voluntary)	☐ Native Hawaiian ☐ American Indian ☐ Other Pacific Islander ☐ Alaska Native ☐ Black/African American ☐ White ☐ Asian

8	**SEX**	☐ Male ☐ Female

9	**A. PARENT/ MOTHER'S NAME AT HER BIRTH** First Full Middle Name Last
	B. PARENT/ MOTHER'S SOCIAL SECURITY NUMBER (See instructions for 9B on Page 3) ☐☐☐ ☐☐ ☐☐☐☐ ☐ Unknown

10	**A. PARENT/ FATHER'S NAME** First Full Middle Name Last
	B. PARENT/ FATHER'S SOCIAL SECURITY NUMBER (See instructions for 10B on Page 3) ☐☐☐ ☐☐ ☐☐☐☐ ☐ Unknown

11	Has the person listed in item 1 or anyone acting on his/her behalf ever filed for or received a Social Security number card before? ☐ Yes (If "yes" answer questions 12-13) ☐ No ☐ Don't Know (If "don't know," skip to question 14.)

12	Name shown on the most recent Social Security card issued for the person listed in item 1	First Full Middle Name Last

13	Enter any different date of birth if used on an earlier application for a card	MM/DD/YYYY

14	**TODAY'S DATE** MM/DD/YYYY	**15**	**DAYTIME PHONE NUMBER** Area Code Number

16	**MAILING ADDRESS** (Do Not Abbreviate)	Street Address, Apt. No., PO Box, Rural Route No. City State/Foreign Country ZIP Code

I declare under penalty of perjury that I have examined all the information on this form, and on any accompanying statements or forms, and it is true and correct to the best of my knowledge.

17	**YOUR SIGNATURE**	**18**	**YOUR RELATIONSHIP TO THE PERSON IN ITEM 1 IS:** ☐ Self ☐ Natural Or Adoptive Parent ☐ Legal Guardian ☐ Other Specify _____

CHAPTER 4

YOUR RETIREMENT BENEFITS UNDER SOCIAL SECURITY

Your retirement benefit is typically the main component of your Social Security benefits. And deciding when to retire is one of the most important lifetime decisions that you will make. The age that you decide to start receiving your Social Security benefits will have a significant impact on the amount of your benefit for the rest of your life. If you decide to apply for Social Security retirement benefits when you reach your full retirement age, then you will receive your full benefit amount. However, your benefit amount is reduced if you start receiving your Social Security retirement benefits before full retirement age, and benefits are increased if postponed beyond full retirement age.

To qualify for Social Security retirement benefits, you will have to earn 40 quarters of coverage by working. You will earn one quarter of coverage with earnings of $1,410 in year 2020. Note that this earnings figure changes each year as it is adjusted for inflation. You can earn up to 4 quarters of coverage in each calendar year. For example, you can get 4 quarters of coverage if you earned $5,640 or more in year 2020. Generally, if you have worked for 10 years or more, you should be eligible for Social Security retirement benefits. However, to maximize the amount of your Social Security retirement benefit you should have 35 years of earnings. Your work can include working for someone else or working for yourself.

The amount of your Social Security retirement benefit is calculated based on a number of factors, including:

1. the number of years you worked in Social Security–covered employment,
2. your age when you start receiving benefits,
3. the amount that you earned each year, and
4. your birthdate.

You should note that the figures have been adjusted for year 2020 such that the maximum Social Security retirement benefit a 65-year-old retiring in 2020 will receive is $2,857 per month (or $34,284 per year). Also, the maximum Social Security retirement benefit a 70-year-old retiring in 2020 will receive is $3,790 per month (or $45,480 per year). In 2020, the average retiree will get about $1,431 per month (about $17,172 per year) in Social Security retirement benefits.

FULL RETIREMENT AGE

The age at which you reach full retirement under Social Security will depend on the year in which you were born. If you were born during or before 1952 or earlier, then you have reached full retirement age and you are already eligible for your full Social Security benefit. The full retirement age is 66 if you were born from 1943 to 1954. The full retirement age increases gradually if you were born from 1955 to 1960 until it reaches 67. For anyone born 1960 or later, full retirement benefits are payable at age 67.

The following chart lists the full retirement age by year of birth.

Age to receive full Social Security benefits:	
Year of birth	*Full retirement age*
1943–1954	66
1955	66 and 2 months
1956	66 and 4 months
1957	66 and 6 months
1958	66 and 8 months
1959	66 and 10 months
1960 and later	67

Note: if you were born on January 1 of any year, then you should refer to the previous year to determine your full retirement age.

Early Retirement

You can start receiving benefits as early as age 62, but your benefits are reduced by about one-half of one percent for each month you start receiving benefits before your full retirement age. For example, if your full retirement age is 66 and six months, and you sign up for Social Security when you are 62, you will only get 72.5 percent of your full benefit. Again, this means if you start receiving your benefit at age 62 in 2020, your benefit would be approximately 27.5 percent lower than it would be at your full retirement age of 66 and 6 months. As the full retirement age increases in future years, the reduction in benefits for early retirement will be larger as the full retirement age increases. So, getting your Social Security retirement benefits early will significantly reduce the amount of your benefit.

The following table from Social Security Administration (at https://www.ssa.gov/OACT/quickcalc/earlyretire.html) illustrates the effect of early retirement, for both a retired worker and his/her spouse. For this illustration, they have used a $1,000 primary insurance amount. With this primary insurance amount and both primary and spouse retiring at their respective normal retirement ages, the primary would receive $1,000 per month and his/her spouse would receive $500 per month. The table shows that retirement at age 62 results in substantial reductions in monthly benefits.

Primary and spousal benefits at age 62 (benefits based on a $1,000 primary insurance amount)

Year of birth[a]	Normal (or full) retirement age	Number of reduction months[b]	Primary		Spouse	
			Amount	Percent reduction	Amount	Percent reduction
1937 or earlier	65	36	$800	20.00%	$375	25.00%
1938	65 and 2 months	38	791	20.83%	370	25.83%
1939	65 and 4 months	40	783	21.67%	366	26.67%
1940	65 and 6 months	42	775	22.50%	362	27.50%
1941	65 and 8 months	44	766	23.33%	358	28.33%
1942	65 and 10 months	46	758	24.17%	354	29.17%
1943–1954	66	48	750	25.00%	350	30.00%
1955	66 and 2 months	50	741	25.83%	345	30.83%
1956	66 and 4 months	52	733	26.67%	341	31.67%
1957	66 and 6 months	54	725	27.50%	337	32.50%
1958	66 and 8 months	56	716	28.33%	333	33.33%
1959	66 and 10 months	58	708	29.17%	329	34.17%
1960 and later	67	60	700	30.00%	325	35.00%

[a] If you are born on January 1, use the prior year of birth.
[b] Applies only if you are born on the 2nd of the month; otherwise the number of reduction months is one less than the number shown.

You may want to stop working before age 62 even if you do not start your Social Security benefit early. Keep in mind, however, that the years in which you have no earnings could calculate to a lower Social Security benefit when you do start to collect your Social Security retirement benefits.

You may have to retire early because of bad health. However, if you cannot work because of health problems you should consider applying for Social Security disability benefits. The disability benefit amount is the same as a full, unreduced retirement benefit. If you are receiving Social Security disability benefits when you reach full retirement age, these disability benefits are converted to retirement benefits. Social Security disability benefits are discussed further in Chapter 7 of this book. You can also get Publication No. 05–10029 (at https://www.ssa.gov/pubs/EN-05-10029.pdf) from Social Security Administration for additional information on disability benefits.

When you have decided to start your Social Security retirement benefits, you can apply for Social Security retirement benefits on their website at www.socialsecurity.gov/benefits.

A sample form for applying for Social Security retirement benefits is also provided in Chapter 10 of this book.

How Benefits Are Affected by Continuing to Work after Receiving Social Security

You can continue to work and still receive retirement benefits. Your earnings during or after the month you reach full retirement age will not reduce your Social Security benefits. Working beyond full retirement age can increase your benefits. However, there will be a reduction in your benefits if your earnings exceed certain limits for the months before you reach your full retirement age.

If you start receiving Social Security retirement benefits before your full retirement age, Social Security Administration will deduct one dollar in benefits for each two dollars in earnings you have above the annual earnings limit. In 2020, the limit is $18,240.

In the year you reach your full retirement age, your benefits are reduced by one dollar for every three dollars you earn over a different annual limit ($48,600 in 2020) until the month you reach full retirement age. However, when you reach full retirement age, you can continue to work, and your Social Security benefit will not be reduced, no matter how much you earn.

These Social Security earnings limits only apply to earnings received while actually working. After your retirement, you may receive payments for work you did before you started getting Social Security benefits. If these payments are for work that you did before your retirement, these payments typically will not affect your Social Security benefit. These special type of payments are not impacted by the earnings limit, and they include bonuses, commissions, accumulated vacation pay, pensions, annuities, IRAs, 401(k)s, investment income, insurance, or deferred compensation and the like. Starting with the month you reach full retirement age, you can get your full benefits no matter how much money you earn.

As indicated earlier there are different earning rules for people who work and receive disability or Supplemental Security Income payments because they must report all their earnings to Social Security Administration regardless of how much they earn. See Chapter 7 of this book for further information on Social Security disability benefits.

There is a special rule which applies to your earnings during your first year of retirement. Under this rule, you can get full Social Security benefits for any month that you earn under a specified monthly earnings limit, regardless of your yearly earnings. More information about how continuing to work affects your benefits is available in Publication No. 05–10069 which you can obtain from the Social Security Administration. This publication has a list of the current annual and monthly earnings limits.

How Delaying Retirement Affects Social Security Benefits

There are two ways in which delaying your retirement and receipt of Social Security benefits can be advantageous to you. Firstly, if you keep working beyond your full retirement age, you can permanently increase your future Social Security benefits. This increase in benefits could happen because of the following:

1. each extra year you work adds another year of earnings to your Social Security record and these could be the years with your highest earnings; and
2. higher lifetime earnings can mean higher benefits when you retire.

Secondly, your Social Security retirement benefit will increase by about 8 percent for each full year you delay receiving Social Security benefits beyond your full retirement age until age 70. This means that your benefit will be adjusted higher the longer you delay starting it up to age 70. This adjustment is usually permanent and it sets the base for the benefits you will receive for the rest of your life. You will also receive annual cost-of-living adjustments, and you may receive higher benefits if you continue to work. So, delaying your retirement and the start of your Social Security retirement payments is one way to maximize your benefits.

When to Start Collecting Your Social Security Retirement Benefits

It is a very important and personal decision in choosing when to retire and start your Social Security retirement benefits. It involves an analysis of many factors including your financial, family, tax, longevity, and health situations.

Most financial advisers say you will need about 70 percent of preretirement income to live comfortably in retirement, including your Social Security benefits, investments, and other personal savings. Remember that Social Security replaces only about 40 percent of a medium-wage earner's preretirement income. This percentage will be lower if you start benefits earlier than your full retirement age and higher if you start benefits after full retirement age. Many advisers say that the best age to start your Social Security retirement benefits is age 70 because this will permanently increase your benefits by 32 percent.

Your longevity and health will greatly impact your retirement decision. Take into account how long you might live when deciding when to start your Social Security retirement benefits. More than a third of the people who are 65 years old will live to age 90 or older. If your parents or grandparents lived into their nineties, there is a good chance that you inherited some of these longevity traits, and you should consider delaying your Social Security benefits to maximize payments for the long term. However, if you are suffering from serious illnesses which shorten your life expectancy, then receiving benefits early may be the best way to optimize your Social Security payments.

Social Security Administration provides a Life Expectancy Calculator at www.socialsecurity.gov/planners/lifeexpectancy.html that you can use to find the average life expectancy for someone your age.

For example, if we assume the full retirement age for a retiree is 66 and he chooses to begin receiving Social Security retirement benefits at age 62, his full retirement age benefit of $1,000 per month may be reduced by about 28 percent, leaving the retiree with about $720 each month. If the retiree instead chooses to begin his benefits at the full retirement age of 66, he would receive the full $1,000 per month benefit, but the break-even point would be age 77 or 11 years from his full retirement age. If you believe that you will live beyond the break-even point, you should consider deferring Social Security retirement benefits until your full retirement age.

Another reason to defer Social Security retirement benefits is if you have not been able to save enough for your retirement. In this case, then you should make every effort to delay your Social Security benefits until after your full retirement age to help increase your future income.

A further reason to delay your benefits is if you are currently in a federal income tax bracket of 22 percent or more. This is because up to 85 percent of Social Security benefits may be taxable.

You should also consider delaying your benefit if you are younger than your full retirement age, and you will continue working while earning more than the annual earnings limit ($18,240 in 2020).

Actuarial advisers suggest that for married couples, the lower-earning spouse should start benefits early (such as age 62) while the higher earner delays as long as possible (such as age 70). If the higher earner dies first, then the surviving spouse can switch to the deceased spouse's much higher benefit.

Besides longevity and health factors, there may be other reasons for starting your Social Security retirement benefits early. For example, you may be unemployed and need Social Security income now for living expenses. Or you may want to collect Social Security retirement benefits early and save and invest these funds for estate planning reasons. Social Security benefits which are collected early and saved can be passed to heirs, whereas heirs generally will receive none of your Social Security benefits after your death.

Medical insurance coverage is another reason to delay retirement and continue working to age 65. If you stop working at age 62 and lose health insurance, you have to get supplemental insurance to bridge the gap until you turn 65 and become eligible for Medicare.

For more information on other factors to consider as you think about when to start receiving Social Security retirement benefits, read "Your Retirement Checklist" (Publication No. 05–10377). It is recommended that you apply for benefits about four months before you want your benefits to start. If you are planning or thinking about retirement, you should visit Social Security's website to use its Retirement Planner at www.socialsecurity.gov/benefits.

CHAPTER 5

FAMILY BENEFITS UNDER SOCIAL SECURITY

If you start receiving Social Security retirement or disability benefits, your family members may also be eligible for payments. As discussed earlier, benefits can be paid to your spouse:

- who is age 62 or older; or
- who is any age if they care for your child younger than age 16 or disabled by age 22 and entitled to Social Security benefits on your record.

Social Security benefits can also be paid to your unmarried children who are younger than age 18; a full-time student in elementary or secondary school between age 18 and 19; or age 18 or older and disabled (the disability must have started before age 22).

Each family member may be eligible for a monthly benefit that is up to half of your retirement or disability benefit amount. However, there is a limit to the total amount of money that can be paid to you and your family. The limit varies, but is generally equal to about 150 to 180 percent of your retirement or disability benefit.

Your ex-spouse may qualify for benefits on your earnings, and they may be able to get benefits even if you are not receiving them. To be eligible for benefits based on your record, your divorced spouse must meet the following criteria:

1. have been married to you for at least 10 years;
2. have been divorced at least two years if you have not filed for benefits;
3. be unmarried;
4. be at least 62 years old; and
5. generally, not be entitled to or eligible for a benefit on their own work that is equal to or higher than half the full amount on your record.

The benefits that your ex-spouse gets will not affect the amount you or your current spouse can get in Social Security benefits.

When you die, your family may be eligible for benefits based on your work. This is because of a program administered by the Social Security Administration which provides survivors benefits. The program is designed to provide benefits to certain dependent individuals when you pass away. Your survivor beneficiaries include your qualifying widow(er), children or parents. More information on Social Security survivor's benefits is given in Chapter 6 of this book.

Your spouse may get a Social Security benefit that is up to 50 percent of your full benefit amount even if your spouse has never worked. It is important to note that your present spouse will not be able to receive spousal benefits based on your record until you have filed for your Social Security retirement benefits. If your spouse is eligible for both their own retirement benefits and spousal benefits, Social Security will pay their own benefits first. However, if the spousal benefit based on your record is a higher amount, then your spouse will get a combined benefit which equals the higher amount. Also, if your birthdate is on or later than January 2, 1954, when you reach full retirement age (and qualify for your own retirement benefits as well as spousal benefits), you can no longer apply for one of the benefits, and delay applying for the other until a later date. Rather, you must apply for both benefits at the same time.

The spousal benefit is reduced if the spouse receives Social Security retirement benefits before they reach full retirement age. The amount of the reduced benefit is determined by the spouse's full retirement age and the age that the spouse begins to receive benefits. And the spouse can start spousal benefits at age 62.

The table below gives an illustration of how Social Security spousal benefits are reduced if the spouse starts to receive these benefits early at age 62.

Percent Amount of Spousal Benefit Based on Regular Entitlement of 50 Percent of Worker's Full Retirement Benefit

Spouse's Full Retirement Age	Percent of Worker's Full Retirement Benefit (If spouse starts to receive benefits at age 62)
65	37.5 percent
66	35 percent
67	32.5 percent

As stated earlier, your spouse can get full benefits at any age if your spouse is taking care of your qualified child who is less than age 16 or disabled before age 22.

Social Security Administration recognizes same-sex couples' marriages in all states, and some non-marital legal relationships (such as some civil unions and domestic partnerships), for purposes of determining entitlement to Social Security benefits, Medicare entitlement, and eligibility and payment amount for Supplemental Security Income (SSI) payments.

Social Security benefits can be paid to your dependent children based on your earnings record. Each dependent child of yours may receive up to 50 percent of your full retirement benefits when you start receiving your Social Security retirement benefits. Your child must be unmarried to qualify for children's benefits regardless of their age. Your child must also be younger than age 18, except if the child is a full-time student up to grade 12 at ages 18 to 19.

Your child can qualify for Social Security benefits at any age if that child suffers from a disability which started before age 22.

There are situations where your stepchild, grandchild, step-grandchild, or an adopted child may be able to receive Social Security benefits. Let Social Security Administration know if you become the parent of a child after you begin receiving benefits, so they can determine if the child is eligible for benefits.

Your parent may be entitled to Social Security benefits based on your Social Security work record. If you provided most of the support for your unmarried parent, then your parent may be able to receive Social Security benefits after your death. Likewise, if you are a parent who received much of your support from a deceased child, you may qualify for Social Security benefits based on your deceased child's earnings record. To qualify for this Social Security parental benefit, you must meet the following conditions:

- you are at least 62 years old;
- you have not remarried since the worker (your child)'s death;

- you are not entitled to your own, higher Social Security benefit; and
- you must submit proof to Social Security Administration within two years of your child's death that you received at least one-half of your financial support from your deceased child at the time of their death.

Always bear in mind that there is a limit to the amount of Social Security benefit that will be paid to you and your family based on a worker's earning record. This limit varies between 150 and 180 percent of the worker's own benefit payment. If the total benefits due to the worker's family are more than this limit, Social Security Administration will reduce the family members benefits, but the worker's own benefits are not affected. For more information about retirement benefits, read "Retirement Benefits" (Publication No. 05–10035) available from Social Security Administration at https://www.ssa.gov/pubs/.

CHAPTER 6

SURVIVOR BENEFITS UNDER SOCIAL SECURITY

Another program administered by the Social Security Administration is Social Security survivors benefits. This is designed to provide benefits to certain dependent individuals if you die. Nearly 6 million people receive Social Security survivor benefits. Your family may qualify for Social Security benefits based on your earnings record when you pass away. These survivor benefits can be a valuable component of financial assistance for family members in need. So, it is important for you and your family to understand the significant survivors benefits that can be provided by Social Security.

A surviving spouse, who is 60 years of age or older, can collect widow or widower benefits based on the deceased spouse's work history. If the surviving spouse is 50 years or older and is also disabled, he or she can qualify for survivors' benefits. Your surviving spouse who is any age can receive survivor's benefits if he or she is taking care of your child, and the child is younger than 16 or is disabled before age 22.

Your unmarried children may qualify for survivor's benefits, if they meet the following criteria:

1. they are less than 18 years of age; or
2. they are between 18 and 19 years old, and are full-time students in an elementary or secondary school; or
3. they are 18 years of age or older and suffering from a disability which started before they were age 22.

Your ex-spouse may be eligible for survivor's benefits based on your earnings record when you die. To qualify for survivor's benefits, your ex-spouse must meet the following requirements:

1. is at least 60 years of age (or 50 if disabled) and have been married to you for at least 10 years; or
2. is any age if they are caring for a child who is eligible for benefits based on your earnings record; and
3. is not currently married, unless the remarriage occurred after age 60 or after age 50 if disabled; and

4. is not entitled to a benefit based on their own work record that is equal or higher than the benefit amount on your record.

However, the benefit payments for other survivors who are receiving benefits based on your record will not be affected by any survivor benefits paid to your ex-spouse.

The benefit that each of your eligible survivors will receive is typically 75–100 percent of your current or expected benefit amount. But, the total amount that will be paid to a family will be limited to about 150–188 percent of your basic Social Security retirement benefit. This means that the survivor benefits paid to widow(er)s, children, and parents of a deceased worker are subject to the maximum family benefit which puts a limit on how much a family can get from Social Security on a single worker's earnings record. Each family member's benefit will be reduced proportionately to meet the maximum family benefit limit.

The chart on page 74 gives a summary of the Survivor Benefits that your family members would receive expressed as a percentage of your actual or expected full retirement benefit. If your surviving beneficiary is entitled to his or her own Social Security benefits, they will receive the higher of their own benefit or your benefit.

Relationship to You	Benefit to Survivor (% of Your Actual or Expected Full Retirement Benefit)
Your widow(er), who is at full retirement age	100%
Your widow(er), who is age 50–59 and disabled	71.5%
Your widow(er), who is at least 60 years old, but who is not at full retirement age _____	71.5%–99%
Your widow(er), who is caring for your child, and this child is under 16 or disabled _____	75%
Your qualifying child	75%
One of your parents	82.5%
Both of your parents	75% each

Another survivor's benefit under Social Security is a one-time payment of $255 which may be made after your death. If they meet certain requirements, this death benefit may be paid to your spouse or minor children.

CHAPTER 7

DISABILITY BENEFITS UNDER SOCIAL SECURITY

You may be eligible for Social Security disability benefits if you are unable to work due to a physical or mental condition. Your condition must be expected to continue for a year or more or expected to result in your death. Many government agencies and insurance companies have disability definitions and rules. However, even if you qualify for disability under other private or governmental agency disability plans, that does not mean that you have met the required disability qualifications for Social Security. Social Security Administration has its own disability rules which are different from other plans or programs. Even a statement from your doctor stating that you have a disability will not automatically make you qualified for Social Security disability benefits. This means that you have to be prepared to prove your disability to Social Security Administration.

If you become disabled, you should file for disability benefits as soon as possible. Typically, Social Security Administration takes several months to review and process a claim for disability. Social Security Administration advises that it may be able to process your claim faster if you have certain information and documentation at the time that you apply for disability benefits. This useful information and documents include the following:

- medical records and treatment dates from your doctors, therapists, hospitals, clinics, and caseworkers;
- your laboratory and other test results;
- the names, addresses, phone, and fax numbers of your doctors, clinics, and hospitals;
- the names of all medications you're taking; and
- the names of your employers and job duties for the last 15 years.

Social Security Administration publishes a manual (commonly called the "Blue Book") which provides a listing of the medical conditions which it considers to be disabilities. This listing manual can be useful to you and your physicians in filing your Social Security disability application. The medical conditions included in the listing manual are given below:

- musculoskeletal problems, such as back injuries
- cardiovascular conditions, such as heart failure or coronary artery disease
- senses and speech issues, such as vision and hearing loss
- respiratory illnesses, such as COPD or asthma
- neurological disorders, such as MS, cerebral palsy, Parkinson's disease, or epilepsy
- mental disorders, such as depression, anxiety, autism, or intellectual disorder
- immune system disorders, such as HIV/AIDS, lupus, and rheumatoid arthritis
- various syndromes, such as Sjogren's Syndrome and Marfan Syndrome
- skin disorders, such as dermatitis
- digestive tract problems, such as liver disease or IBD
- kidney disease and genitourinary problems
- cancer, and
- hematological disorders, such as hemolytic anemias and disorders of bone marrow failure

If you have one of the listed disabilities, then you should see a doctor to get a formal diagnosis of the condition. This diagnosis is just the first step, but it will not automatically qualify you for Social Security disability unless perhaps your doctor diagnoses you with one of the following conditions:

- Amyotrophic Lateral Sclerosis;
- an organ transplant;
- or certain serious cancers, such as esophageal cancer, mucosal melanoma, anaplastic carcinoma of the thyroid gland, or small-cell carcinoma (of the prostate, ovaries, breast, lungs, pleura, intestines, or bladder).

After you have the diagnosis of your medical condition by your doctor, then it has to be determined if your condition meets the specific criteria for that condition, such as for example, hearing loss requires average hearing threshold sensitivity for air conduction 90 decibels or worse in the better ear, coronary artery disease requires 50 percent or more narrowing of a left main coronary artery, blindness requires central visual acuity of 20/200 or less in the better eye with correction, and HIV infection requires an absolute CD4 count of 50 cells/mm3 or less. Be aware that many of the medical condition criteria are very complex and comprehensive and require laboratory or clinical tests.

To speed up the processing of your Social Security disability claim, you should request your doctor to perform any necessary clinical or laboratory tests required in the listing manual. In this way, you will already have all of the required test results in your medical file. Then, you and your doctor can check to see if your test results match or are close to the criteria in the listing manual. If they are, then you should apply for disability. If you cannot get the necessary tests done by your doctor, you can file your disability application and wait for Social Security Administration to do a consultative examination at its own costs. However, having the agency do the consultative examination will slow the processing of your disability application.

Your medical condition does not have to exactly match the requirements in the listing manual for that particular illness or disability. Social Security Administration may give you disability benefits if it considers your aspects of your condition medically equivalent to the criteria in the listing manual. And, even if you do not meet *or* equal the criteria for the listing manual, you may still be eligible for disability benefits, if your condition limits your ability to function so much that you cannot work. Social Security Administration will consider the effect of your condition on your capacity to perform routine daily activities and work. Then, the agency will determine whether there is any kind of job you can safely perform.

Social Security Administration will focus on documentation of the effects that your medical condition has on your ability to work. So, detailed notes in your medical file from your doctor on what activities you are incapable of doing can be very helpful. The agency will consider a number of physical and mental factors in determining your ability to work, such as the following:

- how much you can lift, on a frequent and on an occasional basis;
- how long you can sit or stand;
- how well you can crouch, stoop, or bend;
- how well you can reach forward and overhead;
- how well you can grasp objects or perform dexterous finger movements;
- how well you can hear and see; and
- do you have any serious mental conditions (depression, anxiety, memory problems).

If your doctor has provided little or no information in your medical record as to what functional activities you are not capable of doing, Social Security Administration will likely assume that you do not have any limitations. The agency could then deny disability benefits to you by determining that you should be able to do past work or other work.

To be considered eligible for Social Security disability benefits, you cannot engage in what is known as substantial gainful activity. This means that in year 2020, you cannot collect disability benefits if your earnings exceed $1,260 if you are disabled and $2,110 if you are blind. If you are self-employed you may be able to work up to 45 hours per month and still be eligible for disability benefits (if they are not the only person working for the business and you are not making substantial income).

Here is how you apply for Social Security disability benefits:

- you can file online at www.ssa.gov/applyfordisability (online filing is not available to most SSI applicants);
- you can call the Social Security office at 800-772-1213 for an appointment to apply; or
- you can go to your local Social Security office without an appointment.

Note that, if you are disabled and have little income and few resources, you may be eligible for disability payments through the Supplemental Security Income (SSI) program. For more information about SSI, read "Supplemental Security Income" (SSI) (Publication No. 05–11000) available from Social Security Administration.

More information on disability benefits under Social Security is available from Social Security

Administration's Publication No. 05–10029 and online at https://www.ssa.gov/pubs/index.html?topic =Disability.

CHAPTER 8

TAXES AND SOCIAL SECURITY

The US Social Security system is funded by taxes that you, other workers, and your employers pay into the system depending upon your earnings. You pay Social Security taxes based on your earnings, up to a certain amount. In 2020, the maximum earnings amount for which Social Security taxes are due was $137,700. This means that no additional Social Security payroll tax is owed on earned income in excess of this limit. If you work for an employer, you pay a Social Security tax rate of 6.2 percent and your employer pays a matching 6.2 percent tax rate. If you are self-employed, then you pay the full 12.4 percent Social Security tax rate.

In addition to Social Security taxes, you also pay Medicare taxes on all of your wages or net earnings from self-employment. These taxes are for Medicare health insurance coverage which you will be eligible for at age 65. If you are employed by someone,

then you pay a 1.45 percent Medicare tax on your
entire earnings and your employer pays a matching 1.45 percent Medicare tax. You pay the entire
2.9 percent Medicare tax if you are self-employed.

Taxes on Earned Income

You pay two main types of taxes on earned income, Social Security/Medicare taxes (called FICA,
OASDI, or payroll taxes), and federal and state income taxes. As mentioned earlier, the payroll taxes
that are automatically taken out of your paycheck
have two components: a Social Security tax and a
Medicare tax.

Your Social Security retirement benefits may be
subject to federal income tax if your income exceeds
a certain level. Nearly 40 percent of Social Security
recipients pay taxes on their benefits. If you file your
federal tax return as an "individual, head of household or qualifying widow or widower with a dependent child" and your combined income is between
$25,000 and $34,000, you will likely pay some taxes
on up to 50 percent of your Social Security retirement benefits. If your combined income is more than
$34,000, you may have to pay taxes on up to 85 percent
of your Social Security benefits. Combined income is
defined as the sum of your adjusted gross income plus
nontaxable interest and half of your Social Security
benefits. Combined income does not include any
payments from Roth IRAs.

If you file a joint federal return with your spouse, you may have to pay taxes on 50 percent of your Social Security retirement benefits when you and your spouse have a total combined income that is between $32,000 and $44,000. If your jointly-filed combined income is more than $44,000, up to 85 percent of your Social Security benefits is subject to federal income tax. Also, you will likely pay taxes on your Social Security benefits if you are married and file a separate return. For more information on how your Social Security benefits may be taxed, you can call the toll-free number 1-800-829-3676 at Internal Revenue Service.

Depending on which state you live in, you may also have to pay state income taxes on your Social Security benefits. Thirteen states collect taxes on at least some Social Security income (including Minnesota, North Dakota, Vermont, West Virginia, Colorado, Connecticut, Kansas, Missouri, Montana, Nebraska, New Mexico, Rhode Island and Utah).

The following 37 states (plus Washington, DC) do not tax Social Security benefits: Alabama, Alaska, Arizona, Arkansas, California, Delaware, District of Columbia, Florida, Georgia, Hawaii, Idaho, Illinois, Indiana, Iowa, Kentucky, Louisiana, Maine, Maryland, Massachusetts, Michigan, Mississippi, Nevada, New Hampshire, New Jersey, New York, North Carolina, Ohio, Oklahoma, Oregon, Pennsylvania, South Carolina, South Dakota,

Tennessee, Texas, Virginia, Washington, Wisconsin, Wyoming.

How to Minimize Taxes on Social Security and Other Retirement Income

Before you can make any effective plans for minimizing your federal taxes burden, you should know what tax bracket you are in and what the cutoff points are for the tax brackets for your filing status. Many people mistakenly believe that, when they reach a higher tax bracket, all of their income is taxed at the higher tax rate. However, it is only the income above the threshold for the higher tax bracket that is subject to the higher tax rate. So, the tax brackets have a significant impact on your tax planning strategies.

Effective tax planning also requires that you understand the basics about what is taxable and what is not and know exactly how much taxable income you earn. You may need to work with a professional financial planner for a fuller understanding, but here are some basic principles to keep in mind:

1. Income From Earnings: Generally any income paid to you for work that you performed anywhere in the world is taxable income. This income includes any compensation that you received as an employee, an independent contractor or your part-time business regardless of whether it was salary, hourly wages, bonuses,

commissions, severance pay, stocks and stock options, awards and gifts.

2. Gains From Regular Non-qualified Investments: Ordinarily, all gains from the sale of your normal non-qualified investments are taxable during the year that you sell them. "Non-qualified" investments are generally those that are not approved by the US Internal Revenue Service for tax-deferred or other special tax treatment. The growth that you receive from the sale of these investments are included as part of your annual income. These investments essentially comprise your normal bank checking and savings accounts, credit union accounts, certificates of deposit, stocks, bonds, brokerage accounts, real estate, art, rare coins, vehicles and many more assets.

3. Gains From Individual Retirement Accounts (IRAs): Both traditional and Roth IRAs are "qualified" investments which provide tax-defferred or tax-free, respectively, on the future gains on the investments. Your traditional IRAs contributions are deducted from your income and they are taxable when you withdraw money from these accounts. With the Roth IRAs, you pay a tax when you contribute to these accounts, but your gains are tax-free.

4. Gains From 401(k) Plans: Traditional 401(k) plans are qualified retirement plans set up by

employers that allow employees to save money from their pay and invest on a tax-deferred basis. Your contributions to a traditional 401(k) plan are deducted from your pay and are not included as income on your W-2 statement. Withdrawals from your traditional 401(k) are normally done after retirement and the withdrawals are taxable during the year they are made. For a Roth 401(k) your contributions are deducted from your pay, but the amount is included on your W-2 as income for that year. Your withdrawals from a Roth 401(k) are tax-free.

Remember, depending on your income, up to 85 percent of the money that you receive as Social Security benefits might be taxable income. If your income is less than $25,000 and you are single (or your income is less than $32,000 and you are married), then you will not have to pay taxes on your Social Security benefits. You want to stay below these income levels if you want to keep your Social Security benefits from being taxed. You may be able to achieve this by one or more of these steps:

1. reduce your income by stop working;
2. continue working, but limit your earnings enough to remain below the thresholds;
3. defer your Social Security benefits until you reach age 70 to delay any taxation of these

> benefits and to grow them by 8 percent a year;
> or
> 4. use only your tax-free income such as Roth
>   IRAs or Roth 401(k)s, if needed, to supple-
>   ment your Social Security benefits.

You can reduce your taxable income overall during your retirement if you optimize your investment and withdrawal strategies. If you have traditional IRAs or 40l(k)s and Roth IRAs or Roth 40l(k)s, you should try to withdraw any needed funds firstly from your Roth retirement plans to keep from adding to your taxable income. There are no minimum required distributions from your Roth accounts at age 70½, so this gives you great flexibility in managing your Roth withdrawals. For traditional IRAs or other plans, you are required to take minimum distributions after you reach age 70½ or pay a penalty.

Try to utilize the tax advantages of the income from different types of investments as not all income is treated alike. Understand that the interest payments on bonds and other fixed-income investments are taxed at the higher marginal rates. However, gains on your investments like stocks, real estate, and other capital assets held for more than one year are taxed at the lower capital gains rate, which can be zero, fifteen or twenty percent depending on your income. Keep your year 2020 income below $40,000 if you are single (or $80,000 if you are married and file jointly), and you will pay no taxes on your capital gains. If you have a good mix of taxable and non-taxable accounts, you can take money from your non-taxable accounts when your income is relatively high, and take from your taxable accounts when your income is lower.

You should try to put highly-taxed investments into accounts where taxes are either deferred or tax-free. Investments which pay interest or dividends are taxed at the ordinary income tax rates. Therefore, these investments ideally should be held in tax-deferred or tax-free accounts, such as traditional or Roth IRAs or 401(k)s.

Your conservative investments like stock in big companies and other growth investments should be held in your taxable accounts as the dividends and the gains sale of these investments are taxed at the lower long-term capital gains rate.

Riskier investments such as your stock in small-cap, emerging markets, or pioneering technologies, which have a high potential to make a big gain, should ideally be held in Roth accounts because these accounts are tax-free.

A good source of tax-free income is the gain from the sale of your home. You can exclude up to $250,000 (up to $500,000 if you are married filing jointly) in gain from the sale of your home. The requirements are that you own the home and that you have lived in it as your primary residence for at least two of the past five years. This is a great source of tax-free income that you can repeat over and over.

Some advisers recommend rental real estate as a good investment for retirement. With your rental property, you get to deduct maintenance, insurance, property taxes, depreciation and other expenses, and typically end up no net rental income or a limited loss which can help reduce your ordinary income. And, as mentioned earlier, you can save taxes on gain of $250,000 to $500,000 from the sale of your rental property if you live in it as your primary residence for two out of the past five years.

Another recommendation from financial advisers is to use the years between your regular retirement age and age 70½ to switch money from your traditional IRAs or 401(k)s to Roth accounts. This way you will pay less taxes on your overall retirement income after age 70½ where you could see an increase in your income due to required minimum distributions.

To lower your taxes, you want to be in the lower tax brackets if you can. When you lower your expenses during retirement, this should reduce the amount that you will need to withdraw from your taxable retirement accounts. It will help to keep your taxable income down and you in a lower tax bracket. You also save on taxes if you can keep your income relatively constant over a period of years. Big upward swings in your income will likely mean you have to pay higher taxes overall.

Basically, if you discover that you are paying more in taxes during retirement than you did when you were working, then your financial planning has not been good. This is likely because you are collecting Social Security benefits, have a conservative investment portfolio which pays interest and dividend income, and you are taking required minimum distributions from traditional IRAs and 401(k)s. An effective financial plan can help you optimize income and minimize your taxes.

CHAPTER 9

WHY MANY PEOPLE WILL NEVER GET SOCIAL SECURITY

As mentioned earlier, Social Security is a financial safety net for tens of millions of people. More than 62 million people are receiving Social Security benefits and over 60 percent of them rely on these benefits for at least half of their income. Many more generations of future retirees and their families are also covered by the Social Security program.

Despite the wide reach of Social Security across the population, there are many senior Americans who will never get Social Security benefits. In fact, it is estimated that about 3 percent of the population between the ages of 60 to 90 (approximately 2 million) will never receive any benefits. The Social Security Administration refers to these senior Americans as "never beneficiaries." The agency has essentially grouped the "never beneficiaries" into the four categories of i) infrequent workers, ii) late-arriving immigrants, iii) non-covered workers, and iv) workers who die before receiving benefits. However, other categories of "never beneficiaries" could include ex-patriates, felons and incarcerated persons, divorced spouses with less than 10 years of marriage, self-employed tax evaders, and some delinquent federal debtors.

Over 44 percent of the "never beneficiaries" are infrequent workers who never earn the required 40 work credits to qualify for Social Security benefits. These could be part-time workers or stay-at-home spouses or parents who just did not work the equivalent of 10 years to receive the necessary work credits.

About 37 percent of the "never beneficiaries" include legal immigrants who came to the United States late in life (such as age 50 and beyond) and did not have enough time to earn the 40 work credits needed to receive Social Security benefits. Note that the Social Security program does not provide retired-worker benefits to illegal immigrants or undocumented workers.

Approximately 11 percent of the "never beneficiaries" are described as non-covered workers. This category refers to workers who have worked long enough to otherwise qualify for Social Security benefits, but who do not pay Social Security taxes because they work in non-covered employment, such as state or local government employees, teachers, and railroad employees. However, these non-covered workers usually receive a pension from their government or other employer.

Nearly 7 percent of "never beneficiaries" will die before age 62 retirement (which is the earliest age to start benefits) or pass away after age 62, but before they begin receiving benefits. These are workers who have earned the required 40 work credits, but they do not live long enough to collect their Social Security benefits.

Retirees who move to some foreign countries may not be able to receive their Social Security payments because of restrictions imposed by the United States government. Although many foreign banks will accept direct deposit of Social Security checks, the United States Treasury regulations prohibit payments to persons residing in Cuba or North Korea. But retirees can receive any withheld and future Social Security payments when they move to a country where payments can be sent. The Social Security Administration also cannot make payments to US citizens who live in the countries of Azerbaijan, Belarus, Kazakhstan, Kyrgyzstan, Moldova, Tajikistan, Turkmenistan, Ukraine and Uzbekistan, unless these citizens apply for and receive an exception.

Social Security Administration will not make payments to people who are incarcerated, but their benefits can be reinstated following the month of their release. But a criminal record itself would generally not prevent someone from receiving Social Security benefits.

Divorced ex-spouses who were married for too short of a period of time is another group of people that may not receive Social Security benefits. Typically, an ex-spouse can qualify for a benefit which is equal to one half of the other ex-spouse's Social Security benefits, but only if the marriage lasted for 10 years. However, there are many stay-at-home parents or housewives who did not work to earn Social Security credits of their own. So, if they were divorced before 10 years, they would not be eligible to claim Social Security benefits from their former spouse's earnings record.

People who are delinquent debtors may find that they will receive little or none of their Social Security benefits. A portion of one's Social Security benefits can be withheld by the US Department of Treasury to collect on their past-due obligations such as child support, alimony, federal student loans, federal taxes and other debts owed to federal agencies. How much the government can withhold from a person's Social Security payments will depend on the type of the debt, but for debts owed to the federal government alone, it can take up to 15 percent of your payments until the debt is paid.

If there is no record of a person paying taxes into the Social Security system, then they will not receive benefits. This is why it is always a good idea for workers to check their records at Social Security Administration. Unlike employees whose Social

Security taxes are withheld from their pay, people who are self-employed must file federal tax returns and pay their full self-employment Social Security tax. When a person is a self-employed tax-evader who has not paid his or her Social Security taxes, then they are not entitled to any benefits.

CHAPTER 10

APPLYING FOR SOCIAL SECURITY BENEFITS

When you are ready to begin receiving your Social Security benefits, you should apply for benefits about four months before the date you want your benefits to start. If you are filing for disability or survivors benefits, you should apply as soon as you are eligible. You can apply for benefits on Social Security Administration's website at www.socialsecurity.gov /applyforbenefits or at your local Social Security office.

Even if your retirement is a few months or a few years away, Social Security Administration recommends that you visit its website and utilize its informative retirement planner at www.socialsecurity.gov /benefits to help you map out your retirement plan. You can use the agency's website at www.socialsecurity.gov/estimator for a quick and easy benefit estimate based on your Social Security earnings record.

And, if you want a more detailed benefits calculation, you can get that at www.socialsecurity.gov/planners.

There are certain documents and information that you will need to apply for your benefits. The documents that you must provide will depend on the type of benefit you are filing for. Bear in mind that providing the necessary documents to Social Security Administration up front or as quickly as you can will help the agency process your application and pay your benefits faster. Social Security Administration will not accept photocopies of documents. You are required to have original documents or copies which have been certified by the issuing office or institution.

If you do not have all the required documents you need, Social Security Administration can help to get them. So, do not delay filing your application just because some documents are missing.

Here is a list of some documents you typically need when you sign up for Social Security benefits:

- your Social Security card (or a record of your number);
- your birth certificate;
- your children's birth certificates and Social Security numbers (if you are applying for them);
- proof of US citizenship or lawful immigration status if you (or a child) were not born in the United States;

- your spouse's birth certificate and Social Security number (if they are applying for benefits based on your earnings record);
- your marriage certificate (if you are signing up on a spouse's earnings record or if your spouse is signing up on your earnings record);
- your military discharge papers (if you had military service); and
- your most recent W-2 form (or your tax return, if you are self-employed).

When you apply, Social Security Administration will let you know if you need other documents.

A sample application for applying for Social Security benefits is given here and is also available at your local Social Security office and on their website at www.socialsecurity.gov/applyforbenefits.

Form **SSA-1-BK** (03-2019) UF
Discontinue Prior Editions
Social Security Administration

☐ TEL

Page 1 of 9
OMB No. 0960-0618

APPLICATION FOR RETIREMENT INSURANCE BENEFITS

(Do not write in this space)

I apply for all insurance benefits for which I am eligible under Title II (Federal Old-Age, Survivors, and Disability Insurance) and Part A of Title XVIII (Health Insurance for the Aged and Disabled) of the Social Security Act, as presently amended.

☐ Supplement. If you have already completed an application entitled "APPLICATION FOR WIFE'S OR HUSBAND'S INSURANCE BENEFITS", you need complete only the circled items. All other claimants must complete the entire form.

1.	(a) PRINT your name	FIRST NAME, MIDDLE INITIAL, LAST NAME
	(b) Check (X) whether you are	☐ Male ☐ Female
2.	Enter your Social Security number	

Answer question 3 if English is not your language preference. Otherwise, go to item 4.

3.	Enter the language you prefer to: Speak	Write
4.	(a) Enter your date of birth	Month, Day, Year
	(b) Enter name of city and state, or foreign country where you were born.	
	(c) Was a public record of your birth made before you were age 5?	☐ Yes ☐ No ☐ Unknown
	(d) Was a religious record of your birth made before you were age 5?	☐ Yes ☐ No ☐ Unknown
5.	(a) Are you a U.S. citizen?	☐ Yes (Go to item 7.) ☐ No (Go to item (b).)
	(b) Are you an alien lawfully present in U.S.?	☐ Yes (Go to item (c)) ☐ No (Go to item 6)
	(c) When were you lawfully admitted to the U.S.?	
6.	Enter your full name at birth if different from item 1(a)	FIRST NAME, MIDDLE INITIAL, LAST NAME
7.	(a) Have you used any other name(s)?	☐ Yes (Go to item (b).) ☐ No (Go to item 8.)
	(b) Other names(s) used.	
8.	(a) Have you used any other Social Security number(s)?	☐ Yes (Go to item (b)) ☐ No (Go to item 9.)
	(b) Enter Social Security number(s) used.	

(Over)

Do not answer question 9 if you are one year past full retirement age or older; go to question 10.

9.	(a) Are you, or during the past 14 months have you been, unable to work because of illnesses, injuries or conditions?	☐ Yes	☐ No	
	(b) If "Yes", enter the date you became unable to work.	MONTH, DAY, YEAR		

10.	(a) Have you (or has someone on your behalf) ever filed an application for Social Security, Supplemental Security Income, or hospital or medical insurance under Medicare?	☐ Yes *(If "Yes," answer (b) and (c).)*	☐ No *(If "No," go to item 11.)*	☐ Unknown *(If "Unknown," go to item 11.)*
	(b) Enter name of person(s) on whose Social Security record you filed other application.	FIRST NAME, MIDDLE INITIAL, LAST NAME		
	(c) Enter Social Security number(s) of person named in (b). (If unknown, so indicate.)			

11.	(a) Were you in the active military or naval service (including Reserve or National Guard active duty or active duty for training) after September 7, 1939 and before 1968?	☐ Yes *(If "Yes," answer (b) and (c).)*	☐ No *(If "No," go to item 12.)*
	(b) Enter date(s) of service	Month, Year From:	Month, Year To:
	(c) Have you <u>ever</u> been (or will you be) eligible for monthly benefits from a military or civilian Federal agency? (Include Veterans Administration benefits <u>only</u> if you waived Military retirement pay).	☐ Yes	☐ No

12.	Did you or your spouse (or prior spouse) work in the railroad industry for 5 years or more?	☐ Yes	☐ No

13.	(a) Do you (or your spouse) have Social Security credits (for example based on work or residence) under another country's Social Security system?	☐ Yes *(If "Yes," answer (b) and (c).)*	☐ No *(If "No," go to item 14.)*
	(b) List the country(ies):		
	(c) Are you (or your spouse) filing for foreign Social Security benefits?	☐ Yes	☐ No

Answer question 14 only if you were born January 2, 1924, or later. Otherwise go on to question 15.

14.	(a) Are you entitled to, or do you expect to be entitled to, a pension or annuity (or a lump sum in place of a pension or annuity) based on your work after 1956 not covered by Social Security?	☐ Yes *(If "Yes," answer (b) and (c).)*	☐ No *(If "No," go on to item 15.)*	
			MONTH	YEAR
	(b) I became entitled, or expect to become entitled, beginning			
			MONTH	YEAR
	(c) I became eligible, or expect to become eligible, beginning			

I agree to promptly notify the Social Security Administration if I become entitled to a pension, an annuity, or a lump sum payment based on my employment not covered by Social Security, or if such pension or annuity stops.

15.	Have you been married?	☐ Yes (If "Yes," answer item 16.)	☐ No (If "No," go to item 17.)

16. (a) Give the following information about your current marriage. If not currently married, write "None"
Go on to item 16(b).

Spouse's name (including maiden name)	When (Month, day, year)	Where (Name of City and State)
How marriage ended (If still in effect, write "Not Ended.")	When (Month, day, year)	Where (Name of City and State)
Marriage performed by: ☐ Clergyman or public official ☐ Other (Explain in "Remarks")	Spouse's date of birth (or age)	If spouse deceased, give date of death

Spouse's Social Security number (If none or unknown, so indicate)

(b) Enter information about any other marriage if you:
- Had a marriage that lasted at least 10 years; or
- Had a marriage that ended due to death of your spouse, regardless of duration; or
- Were divorced, remarried the same individual within the year immediately following the year of the divorce, and the combined period of marriage totaled 10 years or more.

Use the "Remarks" space to enter the additional marriage information. If none, write "None." Go on to item 16 (c) if you have a child(ren) who is under age 16 or disabled or handicapped (age 16 or over and disability began before age 22); and you are divorced from the child's other parent, who is now deceased, and the marriage lasted less than 10 years.

Spouse's name (including maiden name)	When (Month, day, year)	Where (Name of City and State)
How marriage ended	When (Month, day, year)	Where (Name of City and State)
Marriage performed by: ☐ Clergyman or public official ☐ Other (Explain in "Remarks")	Spouse's date of birth (or age)	If spouse deceased, give date of death

Spouse's Social Security number (If none or unknown, so indicate)

(c) Enter information about any marriage if you:
- Have a child(ren) who is under age 16 or disabled or handicapped (age 16 or over and disability began before age 22); and
- Were married for less than 10 years to the child's mother or father, who is now deceased; and
- The marriage ended in divorce If none, write "None."

To whom married	When (Month, day, year)	Where (Name of City and State)
How marriage ended	When (Month, day, year)	Where (Name of City and State)
Marriage performed by: ☐ Clergyman or public official ☐ Other (Explain in "Remarks")	Spouse's date of birth (or age)	If spouse deceased, give date of death

Spouse's Social Security number (If none or unknown, so indicate)

Use the 'Remarks' space on page 6 for marriage continuation or explanation.

If your claim for retirement benefits is approved, your children (including adopted children and stepchildren) or dependent grandchildren (including step grandchildren) may be eligible for benefits based on your earnings record.

(Turn to Page 4)

17. List below FULL NAME OF ALL your children (including adopted children, and stepchildren) or dependent grandchildren (including step grandchildren) who are now or were in the past 6 months UNMARRIED and:

- UNDER AGE 18   • AGE 18 TO 19 AND ATTENDING SECONDARY SCHOOL OR ELEMENTARY SCHOOL FULL-TIME
- DISABLED OR HANDICAPPED (age 18 or over and disability began before age 22)

Also list any student who is between the ages of 18 to 23 if such student was both: 1. Previously entitled to Social Security benefits on any Social Security record for August 1981; and 2. In full-time attendance at a post-secondary school.

(IF THERE ARE NO SUCH CHILDREN, WRITE "NONE" BELOW AND GO ON TO ITEM 18.)

18. (a) Did you have wages or self-employment income covered under Social Security in all years from 1978 through last year?

☐ Yes *(If "Yes," go to item 19.)*   ☐ No *(If "No," answer item (b).)*

(b) List the years from 1978 through last year in which you did not have wages or self-employment income covered under Social Security.

19. Enter below the names and addresses of all the persons, companies, or government agencies for whom you have worked this year, last year, and the year before last. **IF NONE, WRITE "NONE" BELOW AND GO ON TO ITEM 20.**

NAME AND ADDRESS OF EMPLOYER (If you had more than one employer, please list them in order beginning with your last (most recent) employer.)	Work Began		Work Ended (If still working, show "Not Ended")	
	Month	Year	Month	Year

(If you need more space, use "Remarks".)

20. THIS ITEM MUST BE COMPLETED, EVEN IF YOU ARE AN EMPLOYEE.
(a) Were you self-employed this year and/or last year?

☐ Yes *(If "Yes," answer (b).)*   ☐ No *(If "No," go to item 21.)*

(b) Check the year or years in which you were self-employed	In what kind of trade or business were you self-employed? (For example, storekeeper, farmer, physician)	Were your net earnings from your trade or business $400 or more? (Check "Yes" or "No")	
☐ This Year		☐ Yes	☐ No
☐ Last Year		☐ Yes	☐ No

21. (a) How much were your total earnings last year?   Amount $

(b) Place an "X" in each block for EACH MONTH of last year in which you did not earn more than *$_____ in wages, and did not perform substantial services in self-employment. These months are exempt months. If no months were exempt months, place an "X" in "NONE". If all months were exempt months, place an "X" in "ALL".

*Enter the appropriate monthly limit after reading the instructions, "How Work Affects Your Benefits".

NONE		ALL	
Jan.	Feb.	Mar.	Apr.
May	Jun.	Jul.	Aug.
Sept.	Oct.	Nov.	Dec.

Form **SSA-1-BK** (03-2019) UF   Page 5 of 9

22.	(a) How much do you expect your total earnings to be this year?	Amount $			

(b) Place an "X" in each block for EACH MONTH of this year in which you did not or will not earn more than *$_____ in wages, and did not or will not perform substantial services in self-employment. These months are exempt months. If no months are or will be exempt months, place an "X" in "NONE". If all months are or will be exempt months, place an "X" in "ALL". *Enter the appropriate monthly limit after reading the instructions, "How Work Affects Your Benefits".	NONE		ALL	
	Jan.	Feb.	Mar.	Apr.
	May	Jun.	Jul.	Aug.
	Sept.	Oct.	Nov.	Dec.

Answer this item ONLY if you are now in the last 4 months of your taxable year (Sept., Oct., Nov., and Dec., if your taxable year is a calendar year).

23.	(a) How much do you expect to earn next year?	Amount $			

(b) Place an "X" in each block for EACH MONTH of next year in which you do not expect to earn more than *$_____ in wages, and do not expect to perform substantial services in self-employment. These months will be exempt months. If no months are expected to be exempt months, place an "X" in "NONE". If all months are expected to be exempt months, place an "X" in "ALL". *Enter the appropriate monthly limit after reading the instructions, "How Work Affects Your Benefits".	NONE		ALL	
	Jan.	Feb.	Mar.	Apr.
	May	Jun.	Jul.	Aug.
	Sept.	Oct.	Nov.	Dec.

24.	If you use a fiscal year, that is, a taxable year that does not end December 31 (with income tax return due April 15), enter here the month your fiscal year ends. _____ (Month)

DO NOT ANSWER ITEM 25 IF YOU ARE FULL RETIREMENT AGE AND 6 MONTHS OR OLDER. YOU MAY HAVE MORE FILING OPTIONS; A SOCIAL SECURITY REPRESENTATIVE WILL CONTACT YOU TO DISCUSS ADDITIONAL INFORMATION THAT MAY HELP YOU DECIDE WHEN TO START YOUR BENEFIT. GO TO ITEM 26.

PLEASE READ CAREFULLY THE INFORMATION ON THE BOTTOM OF PAGE 9 AND ANSWER ONE OF THE FOLLOWING ITEMS:

25.	(a) ☐ I want benefits beginning with the earliest possible month, and will accept an age-related reduction.
	(b) ☐ I am full retirement age (or will be within 12 months), and want benefits beginning with the earliest possible month providing there is no permanent reduction in my ongoing monthly benefits.
	(c) ☐ I want benefits beginning with _____ .

MEDICARE INFORMATION

If this claim is approved and you are still entitled to benefits at age 65, or you are within 3 months of age 65 or older you could automatically receive Medicare Part A (Hospital Insurance) and Medicare Part B (Medical Insurance) coverage at age 65. If you live in Puerto Rico or a foreign country, you are not eligible for automatic enrollment in Medicare Part B, and you will need to contact Social Security to request enrollment.

COMPLETE ITEM 26 ONLY IF YOU ARE WITHIN 3 MONTHS OF AGE 65 OR OLDER

Medicare Part B (Medical Insurance) helps cover doctor's services and outpatient care. It also covers some other services that Medicare Part A does not cover, such as some of the services of physical and occupational therapists and some home health care. If you enroll in Medicare Part B, you will have to pay a monthly premium. The amount of your premium will be determined when your coverage begins. In some cases, your premium may be higher based on information about your income we receive from the Internal Revenue Service. Your premiums will be deducted from your monthly Social Security, Railroad Retirement, or Office of Personnel Management benefits you receive. If you do not receive any of these benefits, you will get a letter explaining how to pay your premiums. You will also get a letter if there is any change in the amount of your premium.

If you do not sign up for Part B when you are first eligible, you may have to pay a late enrollment penalty for as long as you have Part B. Your monthly premium for Part B may go up 10% for each full 12-month period that you could have had Part B, but did not sign up for it. Also, you may have to wait until the General Enrollment Period (January 1 to March 31) to enroll in Part B, and coverage will start July 1 of that year.

You can also enroll in a Medicare prescription drug plan (Part D). To learn more about the Medicare prescription drug plans and when you can enroll, visit www.medicare.gov or call 1-800-MEDICARE (1-800-633-4227; TTY 1-877-486-2048). Medicare can also tell you about agencies in your area that can help you choose your prescription drug coverage. The amount of your premium varies based on the prescription drug plan provider. The amount you pay for Part D coverage may be higher than the listed plan premium, based on information about your income we receive from the Internal Revenue Service.

If you have limited income and resources, we encourage you to apply for the Extra Help that is available to assist you with Medicare prescription drug costs. The Extra Help can pay the monthly premiums, annual deductibles, and prescription co-payments. To learn more or apply, please visit www.socialsecurity.gov, call 1-800-772-1213 (TTY 1-800-325-0778) or visit the nearest Social Security office.

| 26. | Do you want to enroll in Medicare Part B (Medical insurance)? | ☐ Yes | ☐ No |
| 27. | If you are within 2 months of age 65 or older, blind or disabled, do you want to file for Supplemental Security Income? | ☐ Yes | ☐ No |

REMARKS (You may use this space for any explanations. If you need more space, attach a separate sheet.)

Form **SSA-1-BK** (03-2019) UF

I declare under penalty of perjury that I have examined all the information on this form, and on any accompanying statements or forms, and it is true and correct to the best of my knowledge. I understand that anyone who knowingly gives a false statement about a material fact in this information, or causes someone else to do so, commits a crime and may be subject to a fine or imprisonment.

SIGNATURE OF APPLICANT

SIGNATURE *(First Name, Middle Initial, Last Name) (Write in ink.)*

Date (Month, day, year)	Telephone number(s) at which you may be contacted during the day

Direct Deposit Payment Information *(Financial Institution)*

Routing Transit Number	Account Number		
		☐ Checking	☐ Enroll in Direct Express
		☐ Savings	☐ Direct Deposit Refused

Applicant's Mailing Address *(Number and street, Apt No., P.O. Box, or Rural Route)*
(Enter Residence Address in "Remarks," if different.)

City and State	ZIP Code	County (if any) in which you now live

Witnesses are required ONLY if this application has been signed by mark (X) above. If signed by mark (X), two witnesses who know the applicant must sign below, giving their full addresses. Also, print the applicant's name in the Signature block.

1. Signature of Witness	2. Signature of Witness

Address (Number and Street, City, State and ZIP Code)	Address (Number and Street, City, State and ZIP Code)

Form **SSA-1-BK** (03-2019) UF

RECEIPT FOR YOUR CLAIM FOR SOCIAL SECURITY RETIREMENT INSURANCE BENEFITS

	BEFORE YOU RECEIVE A NOTICE OF AWARD	SSA OFFICE	DATE CLAIM RECEIVED
TELEPHONE NUMBER(S) TO CALL IF YOU HAVE A QUESTION OR SOMETHING TO REPORT	AFTER YOU RECEIVE A NOTICE FOF AWARD		

Your application for Social Security benefits has been received and will be processed as quickly as possible.

You should hear from us within_____ days after you have given us all the information we requested. Some claims may take longer if additional information is needed.

In the meantime, if you change your address, or if

there is some other change that may affect your claim, you - or someone for you - should report the change. The changes to be reported are listed on page 9.

Always give us your claim number when writing or telephoning about your claim.

If you have any questions about your claim, we will be glad to help you.

CLAIMANT	SOCIAL SECURITY CLAIM NUMBER

Privacy Act Statement
Collection and Use of Information

Sections 202, 205, and 223 of the Social Security Act, as amended, allow us to collect this information. Furnishing us this information is voluntary. However, failing to provide all or part of the information may prevent us from making an accurate and timely decision concerning your or a dependent's eligibility to benefit payments.

We will use the information you provide to help us determine your or a dependent's eligibility for benefit payments. We may also share the information for the following purposes, called routine uses:

1. To contractors and other Federal agencies, as necessary, for the purpose of assisting the Social Security Administration (SSA) in the efficient administration of its programs.

2. To student volunteers, individuals working under a personal services contract, and other workers who technically do not have the status of Federal employees, when they are performing work for SSA, as authorized by law, and they need access to personally identifiable information in SSA records in order to perform their assigned agency functions.

In addition, we may share this information in accordance with the Privacy Act and other Federal laws. For example, where authorized, we may use and disclose this information in computer matching programs, in which our records are compared with other records to establish or verify a person's eligibility for Federal benefit programs and for repayment of incorrect or delinquent debts under these programs.

A list of additional routine uses is available in our Privacy Act System of Records Notices (SORN) 60-0059, entitled Earnings Recording and Self-Employment Income System and 60-0089, entitled Claims Folders System. Additional information and a full listing of all our SORNs are available on our website at www.socialsecurity.gov/foia/bluebook.

Paperwork Reduction Act Statement - This information collection meets the requirements of 44 U.S.C. § 3507, as amended by section 2 of the Paperwork Reduction Act of 1995. You do not need to answer these questions unless we display a valid Office of Management and Budget control number. We estimate that it will take about 11 minutes to read the instructions, gather the facts, and answer the questions. **SEND OR BRING THE COMPLETED FORM TO YOUR LOCAL SOCIAL SECURITY OFFICE. You can find your local Social Security office through SSA's website at www.socialsecurity.gov. Offices are also listed under U. S. Government agencies in your telephone directory or you may call Social Security at 1-800-772-1213 (TTY 1-800-325-0778).** *You may send comments on our time estimate above to: SSA, 6401 Security Blvd, Baltimore, MD 21235-6401. Send only comments relating to our time estimate to this address, not the completed form.*

CHANGES TO BE REPORTED AND HOW TO REPORT
Failure to report may result in overpayments that must be repaid, and in possible monetary penalties

- You change your mailing address for checks or residence. (*To avoid delay in receipt of checks you should ALSO file a regular change of address notice with your post office.*)

- Your citizenship or immigration status changes.

- You go outside the U.S.A. for 30 consecutive days or longer.

- Any beneficiary dies or becomes unable to handle benefits.

- Work Changes - On your application you told us you expect total earnings for_____ to be $_____.

(Year)

  You ☐ (are) ☐ (are not) earning wages of more than $_____ a month.

  You ☐ (are) ☐ (are not) self-employed rendering substantial services in your trade or business.

  (Report AT ONCE if this work pattern changes)

- You are confined to a jail, prison, penal institution or correctional facility for more than 30 continuous days for conviction of a crime, or you are confined for more than 30 continuous days to a public institution by a court order in connection with a crime.

- You have an unsatisfied warrant for more than 30 continuous days for your arrest for a crime or attempted crime that is a felony of flight to avoid prosecution or confinement, escape from custody and flight-escape. In most jurisdictions that do not classify crimes as felonies, this applies to a crime that is punishable by death or imprisonment for a term exceeding one year (regardless of the actual sentence imposed).

- You have an unsatisfied warrant for more than 30 continuous days for a violation of probation or parole under Federal or State law.

- You become entitled to a pension, an annuity, or a lump sum payment based on your employment not covered by Social Security, or if such pension or annuity stops.

- Your stepchild is entitled to benefits on your record and you and the stepchild's parent divorce. Stepchild benefits are not payable beginning with the month after the month the divorce becomes final.

- Custody Change - Report if a person for whom you are filing or who is in your care dies, leaves your care or custody, or changes address.

- Change of Marital Status - Marriage, divorce, annulment of marriage.

- If you become the parent of a child (including an adopted child) after you have filed your claim, let us know about the child so we can decide if the child is eligible for benefits. Failure to report the existence of these children may result in the loss of possible benefits to the child(ren).

HOW TO REPORT

You can make your reports online, by telephone, mail, or in person, whichever you prefer.

If you are awarded benefits, and one or more of the above change(s) occur, you should report by:

- Visiting the section "my Social Security" at our web site at www.socialsecurity.gov.

- Calling us TOLL FREE at 1-800-772-1213.

- If you are deaf or hearing impaired, calling us TOLL FREE at TTY 1-800-325-0778; or

- Calling, visiting or writing your local Social Security office at the phone number and address shown on your claim receipt.

For general information about Social Security, visit our web site at www.socialsecurity.gov.

For those under full retirement age, the law requires that a report of earnings be filed with SSA within 3 months and 15 days after the end of any taxable year in which you earn more than the annual exempt amount. You may contact SSA to file a report. Otherwise, SSA will use the earnings reported by your employer(s) and your self-employment tax return (if applicable) as the report of earnings required by law, to adjust benefits under the earnings test. It is your responsibility to ensure that the information you give concerning your earnings is correct. You must furnish additional information as needed when your benefit adjustment is not correct based on the earnings on your record.

PLEASE READ THE FOLLOWING INFORMATION CAREFULLY BEFORE YOU ANSWER QUESTION 25.

- If you are under full retirement age, retirement benefits cannot be payable to you for any month before the month in which you file your claim.

- If you are over full retirement age, retirement benefits may be payable to you for some months before the month in which you file this claim.

- If your first month of entitlement is prior to full retirement age, your benefit rate will be reduced. However, if you do not actually receive your full benefit amount for one or more months before full retirement age because benefits are withheld due to your earnings, your benefit will be increased at full retirement age to give credit for this withholding. Thus, your benefit amount at full retirement age will be reduced only if you receive one or more full benefit payments prior to the month you attain full retirement age.

  - Delayed retirement credits may be added to your benefits if you request them to start when you are full retirement age or older.

  - Please visit our www.ssa.gov web site to use the Retirement Estimator to get a personal estimate of how much your benefits will be at different ages. In addition, our web site provides information about other things you should think about when you make your decision about when to begin your benefits.

CHAPTER 11

HOW SOCIAL SECURITY BENEFITS ARE PAID

Social Security Administration does not pay benefits by check or other paper instruments. To get your Social Security benefits, you have to receive the payments electronically. One of the ways to receive payment of your benefits is through direct deposit to your account at a bank or other financial institution. The direct deposit is an easy, timely, and safe means to get your Social Security payments. To set up direct deposit with Social Security you will need your account number and the routing number of your financial institution. You should find this information on the front of the checks in your checkbook or perhaps on your account statement. Make sure that this information is accurate to ensure that your payments are deposited into the correct account.

Another way that you can choose to receive your Social Security is on a prepaid debit card. For this, you can sign up for the Direct Express® card program. With the Direct Express® card, your Social Security payments will go directly to your card account. You can use the card to make purchases, pay bills, or get cash at thousands of locations. You can quickly and easily sign up for the card by calling the Direct Express® toll-free hotline at 1-800-333-1795. The Social Security Administration can assist you in signing up for this card.

Another payment choice you can consider is an electronic transfer account. With this low-cost federally insured account, you can enjoy the security and convenience of automatic payments. An electronic transfer account is basically a bank account for federal payment recipients who do not have checking or savings accounts. Instead of receiving your Social Security payments by check, an electronic transfer account will enable you to receive your payments by direct deposit. This method is much faster, more convenient and more secure than receiving payment by check. You can set up an electronic transfer account at those banks, or savings and loans and credit unions that have registered with the US Treasury as providers. You cannot write out checks on an electronic transfer account, but you can usually withdraw funds from the account over the counter, at an ATM, or through debit card purchases.

Some further benefits of an electronic transfer account are:

- no minimum balance
- a maximum service charge of $3 per month
- at least four free cash withdrawals and balance confirmations per month
- automatic direct deposit of Social Security and other federal payments
- the potential for the account holder to deposit funds from other sources
- delivery of an account summary statement each month.

Social Security Administration operates a representative payee program and may make your benefits payments to this representative payee. A representative payee is a person, agency, organization or institution selected by Social Security Administration to manage your benefits when they determine that you are unable to do so yourself (or direct others to do it for you). The agency must evaluate medical and other evidence about your ability to manage your Social Security benefits before appointing a representative payee. The people who must have a representative payee are i) most children under the age of 18, ii) people who are legally incompetent, and iii) people that the agency determines are not capable of managing or directing their benefits payments.

To serve as your representative payee, Social Security Administration requires that the payee be one of the following:

- someone who is concerned with your welfare (usually a parent, spouse, close relative, guardian, or friend);
- an institution, such as a nursing home or health care provider;
- a public or nonprofit agency, social service agency, or financial organization;
- providers or administrative officers at homeless shelters; or
- a community-based nonprofit agency that has been approved by Social Security Administration to charge a fee for its service as a payee.

The representative payee's duty is to understand your needs and to use the benefits in your best interests, including your current basic needs for food, clothing, housing, medical care, and personal comfort items. Each year, Social Security Administration will require that certain representative payees complete an accounting report showing how they spent and saved the money they received for you. Your representative payee's authority is limited to matters between you and Social Security Administration; a representative payee has no authority to enter into any binding contracts on your behalf. Note that your power of attorney does not give someone authority to act as your representative payee. And, you or your representative payee may, at any time, request that Social Security Administration change or terminate the payee arrangement.

For more information on representative payees you can read Social Security Administration's publication "When a Representative Payee Manages Your Money" at www.ssa.gov/pubs/EN-05-10097.pdf.

The Social Security Administration can expedite benefits in situations requiring these types of payments:

- presumptive disability or presumptive blindness payment;
- immediate payment;
- expedited reinstatement cases; and
- emergency advance payment. For example, the agency can make an emergency advance payment to new applicants who face a financial emergency and who are due SSI benefits that are delayed or not received.

You can request that Social Security Administration suspend your retirement benefit payments at any time between your full retirement age and age 70. This request can be done in writing, over the phone, or orally at a Social Security office. If you suspend your benefit payments, they will start automatically the month you reach age 70. You can change your decision to suspend your benefit payments at any time by notifying Social Security Administration (in writing or orally) when you want your benefits reinstated. You can also request back payment for any or all of the months when your benefit payments were suspended.

Be aware that if you voluntarily suspend your retirement benefits and you have others who receive benefits on your record, they (except for your divorced spouse) will not be able to receive benefits for the same period that your benefits are suspended. Further, if you voluntarily suspend your retirement benefit, any benefits that you receive on someone else's record will also be suspended. And if you are on Medicare, your Part B premiums cannot be deducted from your suspended Social Security benefits and you will have to make other arrangements to pay these premiums.

You can change your mind about receiving Social Security benefits and withdraw your application for benefits. But, you can withdraw your Social Security application only if it has been less than 12 months since you were first entitled to and started your benefits. To withdraw your application, you must make a written request to withdraw and repay any benefits payments that you and your family received. If you withdraw your application, you can re-apply at a future date.

Your Social Security benefits are paid to you the month after they are due. For example, your benefits for January of each year are paid in February. You will receive your Social Security retirement benefit payments on the 3rd of each month if i) you started receiving your Social Security benefits before May 1997 or ii) you are receiving Supplemental Security Insurance and Social Security benefits. Otherwise, you will receive your Social Security benefit payments as follows:

- on the 2nd Wednesday of each month, if your birthdate is on the days 1–10 of the month;
- on the 3rd Wednesday of each month, if your birthdate is on days 11–20 of the month; and
- on the 4th Wednesday of each month, if your birthdate is on days 21–31 of the month.

Calendars which show the specific schedule of Social Security benefit payments for years 2020 and 2021 are given at the end of this chapter.

Note that if you live outside of the United States, there are a number of Social Security Field Offices and American embassies and consulates who have specially trained personnel to assist you in seeking Social Security services. You can access information to contact your Social Security and consular staff by locating your country using the web address: https://www.ssa.gov/foreign/foreign.htm .

Schedule of Social Security Benefit Payments 2020

JANUARY 2020						
S	M	T	W	T	F	S
			1	2	3	4
5	6	7	8	9	10	11
12	13	14	15	16	17	18
19	20	21	22	23	24	25
26	27	28	29	30	31	

FEBRUARY 2020						
S	M	T	W	T	F	S
						1
2	3	4	5	6	7	8
9	10	11	12	13	14	15
16	17	18	19	20	21	22
23	24	25	26	27	28	29

MARCH 2020						
S	M	T	W	T	F	S
1	2	3	4	5	6	7
8	9	10	11	12	13	14
15	16	17	18	19	20	21
22	23	24	25	26	27	28
29	30	31				

APRIL 2020						
S	M	T	W	T	F	S
			1	2	3	4
5	6	7	8	9	10	11
12	13	14	15	16	17	18
19	20	21	22	23	24	25
26	27	28	29	30		

MAY 2020						
S	M	T	W	T	F	S
					1	2
3	4	5	6	7	8	9
10	11	12	13	14	15	16
17	18	19	20	21	22	23
24	25	26	27	28	29	30
31						

JUNE 2020						
S	M	T	W	T	F	S
	1	2	3	4	5	6
7	8	9	10	11	12	13
14	15	16	17	18	19	20
21	22	23	24	25	26	27
28	29	30				

JULY 2020						
S	M	T	W	T	F	S
			1	2	3	4
5	6	7	8	9	10	11
12	13	14	15	16	17	18
19	20	21	22	23	24	25
26	27	28	29	30	31	

AUGUST 2020						
S	M	T	W	T	F	S
						1
2	3	4	5	6	7	8
9	10	11	12	13	14	15
16	17	18	19	20	21	22
23	24	25	26	27	28	29
30	31					

SEPTEMBER 2020						
S	M	T	W	T	F	S
		1	2	3	4	5
6	7	8	9	10	11	12
13	14	15	16	17	18	19
20	21	22	23	24	25	26
27	28	29	30			

OCTOBER 2020						
S	M	T	W	T	F	S
				1	2	3
4	5	6	7	8	9	10
11	12	13	14	15	16	17
18	19	20	21	22	23	24
25	26	27	28	29	30	31

NOVEMBER 2020						
S	M	T	W	T	F	S
1	2	3	4	5	6	7
8	9	10	11	12	13	14
15	16	17	18	19	20	21
22	23	24	25	26	27	28
29	30					

DECEMBER 2020						
S	M	T	W	T	F	S
		1	2	3	4	5
6	7	8	9	10	11	12
13	14	15	16	17	18	19
20	21	22	23	24	25	26
27	28	29	30	31		

Benefits paid on	Birth date on
Second Wednesday	1st – 10th
Third Wednesday	11th – 20th
Fourth Wednesday	21st – 31st

Supplemental Security Income (SSI)

Social Security benefits prior to May 1997; or if receiving both Social Security and SSI, Social Security is paid on the third of the month.

If you don't receive your payment on the expected date, please allow three additional mailing days before contacting Social Security.

Securing today and tomorrow

SocialSecurity.gov

Social Security Administration
Publication No. 05-10031
ICN 456100 I Unit of Issue — HD (one hundred)
January 2020 (Recycle prior editions)
Schedule of Social Security Benefit Payments 2020
Produced and published at U.S. taxpayer expense

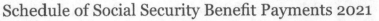

Schedule of Social Security Benefit Payments 2021

JANUARY 2021

S	M	T	W	T	F	S
					1	2
3	4	5	6	7	8	9
10	11	12	13	14	15	16
17	18	19	20	21	22	23
24	25	26	27	28	29	30
31						

FEBRUARY 2021

S	M	T	W	T	F	S
	1	2	3	4	5	6
7	8	9	10	11	12	13
14	15	16	17	18	19	20
21	22	23	24	25	26	27
28						

MARCH 2021

S	M	T	W	T	F	S
	1	2	3	4	5	6
7	8	9	10	11	12	13
14	15	16	17	18	19	20
21	22	23	24	25	26	27
28	29	30	31			

APRIL 2021

S	M	T	W	T	F	S
				1	2	3
4	5	6	7	8	9	10
11	12	13	14	15	16	17
18	19	20	21	22	23	24
25	26	27	28	29	30	

MAY 2021

S	M	T	W	T	F	S
						1
2	3	4	5	6	7	8
9	10	11	12	13	14	15
16	17	18	19	20	21	22
23	24	25	26	27	28	29
30	31					

JUNE 2021

S	M	T	W	T	F	S
		1	2	3	4	5
6	7	8	9	10	11	12
13	14	15	16	17	18	19
20	21	22	23	24	25	26
27	28	29	30			

JULY 2021

S	M	T	W	T	F	S
				1	2	3
4	5	6	7	8	9	10
11	12	13	14	15	16	17
18	19	20	21	22	23	24
25	26	27	28	29	30	31

AUGUST 2021

S	M	T	W	T	F	S
1	2	3	4	5	6	7
8	9	10	11	12	13	14
15	16	17	18	19	20	21
22	23	24	25	26	27	28
29	30	31				

SEPTEMBER 2021

S	M	T	W	T	F	S
			1	2	3	4
5	6	7	8	9	10	11
12	13	14	15	16	17	18
19	20	21	22	23	24	25
26	27	28	29	30		

OCTOBER 2021

S	M	T	W	T	F	S
					1	2
3	4	5	6	7	8	9
10	11	12	13	14	15	16
17	18	19	20	21	22	23
24	25	26	27	28	29	30
31						

NOVEMBER 2021

S	M	T	W	T	F	S
	1	2	3	4	5	6
7	8	9	10	11	12	13
14	15	16	17	18	19	20
21	22	23	24	25	26	27
28	29	30				

DECEMBER 2021

S	M	T	W	T	F	S
			1	2	3	4
5	6	7	8	9	10	11
12	13	14	15	16	17	18
19	20	21	22	23	24	25
26	27	28	29	30	31	

Benefits paid on	Birth date on
Second Wednesday	1st – 10th
Third Wednesday	11th – 20th
Fourth Wednesday	21st – 31st

Supplemental Security Income (SSI)

Social Security benefits prior to May 1997; or if receiving both Social Security and SSI, Social Security is paid on the third of the month.

If you don't receive your payment on the expected date, please allow three additional mailing days before contacting Social Security.

Securing today and tomorrow

SocialSecurity.gov

Social Security Administration
Publication No. 05-10031
ICN 456100 I Unit of Issue — HD (one hundred)
January 2020 (Recycle prior editions)
Schedule of Social Security Benefit Payments 2021
Produced and published at U.S. taxpayer expense

CHAPTER 12

YOUR RIGHT TO APPEAL DECISIONS BY THE SOCIAL SECURITY ADMINISTRATION

(Source: US Social Security Administration)

If you disagree with a decision made on your Social Security claim, you can appeal it. You and your representative, if you have one, can look at the evidence in your case file and submit new evidence. Additional evidence should be submitted at least 5 days before the hearing. You may also file a request for extension of time to file a request for review online at www .socialsecurity.gov/disability/appeals.

Submit any additional evidence you want the Administrative Law Judge to consider as soon as possible. If you do not have it when you request a hearing, send it to the Administrative Law Judge as soon as you can. If your case is electronic, evidence can be faxed into the claim file using a special fax number and bar code provided by the hearing office or sent by your representative through Electronic Records Express (ERE) at www.socialsecurity.gov/ere.

You can handle your own appeal with free help from Social Security, or you can choose to have a representative help you. Social Security Administration can give you information about organizations that can help you find a representative. For more information about selecting a representative, read "Your Right to Representation" (Publication No. 05–10075).

You can question the decision Social Security Administration makes on your case. If you are eligible for Social Security or Supplemental Security Income benefits, you want to get them on time and in the right amount. After the agency decides whether or not you are eligible for benefits, or that they will stop your benefits, or change the amount, they will send you a letter explaining the decision. If you do not agree with the decision, you have the right to appeal it. When you ask for an appeal, Social Security may review the entire decision, including those parts which were favorable to you.

There are four steps of appeal and they are as follows:

1. Reconsideration—You may request a review or reconsideration of your case if you disagree with the first decision. Then, a person who did not make the first decision will decide your case again.

2. Administrative Law Judge Hearing—You may request a hearing before an Administrative Law Judge if you disagree with the reconsideration decision. You may request a hearing via the Internet at www.socialsecurity.gov/disability/appeals.

3. Appeals Council Action—You may request the Appeals Council to review your case if you disagree with the Administrative Law Judge's action. You may file a request for review via the Internet at www.socialsecurity.gov/disability/appeals.

4. Federal Court Action—If you disagree with the Appeals Council's decision, or if the Appeals Council decides not to review your case, you can file a civil suit in a federal district court. This is the last level of the appeals process. Currently, this process is not available online. To learn more about this process, visit Federal Court Review Process.

If you have already been through Step #1 of the appeals process, you will have received a letter explaining Social Security Administration's reconsideration decision. Later in this chapter, you will get an explanation of the other appeals steps.

You may have a representative such as a lawyer, friend, or other qualified person to represent you. If you have a representative, you may have to pay his or her fees. For more information about representation and about the fees a representative may charge, read "Your Right to Representation" (Publication No. 05–10075).

If you decide to have a representative, you should let Social Security Administration know in writing as soon as possible. To do this, use Form SSA-1696-U4, Appointment of Representative, available at www.socialsecurity.gov or at any Social Security office.

How to Request a Hearing or Appeals Council Review

You or your representative may request a hearing by an Administrative Law Judge in the Office of Hearings Operations. At the time of your request, the Administrative Law Judge will not have had any part in your case. However, if you think that after hearing your case the Administrative Law Judge's decision is wrong, you may request that the Appeals Council, which is located within our Office of Analytics, Review, and Oversight, review the judge's action. Your request must be in writing. Your Social Security office can help you fill out the special form for either a hearing or an Appeals Council review at any Social Security office, or you can write us a letter. Additionally, you may file an appeal online by visiting www.socialsecurity.gov/disability/appeals.

Generally, you have 60 days after you receive the notice of the decision to ask for any type of appeal. In counting the 60 days, it is presumed that you received the notice five days after it was mailed unless you can show that you received it later.

If you do not appeal on time, the Administrative Law Judge or the Appeals Council may dismiss your appeal. This means that you may not be eligible for the next step in the appeal process and that you may also lose your right to any further review. You must have a good reason if you wait more than 60 days to request an appeal. If you file an appeal after the deadline, you must explain the reason you are late and request that we extend the time limit.

The representatives in the Social Security office can explain this further and help you file a written request to extend the time limit.

After you request a hearing, your Social Security office sends your case file to the Administrative Law Judge's office. Although the Administrative Law Judge attempts to schedule all hearings promptly, there may be some delay if there are many requests ahead of yours or because of travel schedules. At least 75 days before the hearing, the Administrative Law Judge will send you a notice telling you the date, time, and place of the hearing. The Administrative Law Judge usually holds the hearing within 75 miles of your home.

You must let the Social Security office know in writing when requesting a hearing if you do not wish to appear or cannot appear at the hearing. Give your reasons, and ask the Administrative Law Judge to make a decision based on the evidence in your file and any new evidence. However, if your claim involves "disability," you may want to explain how your medical problems limit your activities and prevent you from working.

The Administrative Law Judge may decide that your presence at the hearing will be helpful, especially if only you can best explain certain facts. If so, he or she may schedule a hearing even if you asked not to be present. You should go to your scheduled hearing.

If travel arrangements will present a problem for you, tell the Social Security office when you request a hearing or as soon as possible after that. If you want to appear at a hearing but are unable to travel because of your health, submit a doctor's report with your request for a hearing, explaining why you cannot travel. If Social Security Administration is using video hearing equipment in your area, they may schedule a video appearance for you.

If the Administrative Law Judge schedules a hearing, you and your representative, if you have one, should attend. It is very important that you attend a scheduled hearing. If for any reason you cannot attend, contact the Administrative Law Judge as soon as possible before the hearing and state the reason.

The Administrative Law Judge will reschedule the hearing if you have provided a good reason. If you do not go to a scheduled hearing and the Administrative Law Judge decides that you do not have a good reason for not going, your request for a hearing may be dismissed.

Administrative Law Judge Hearing

The Administrative Law Judge explains the issues in your case and may question you and any witnesses at the hearing. You may bring witnesses to your hearing. The Administrative Law Judge may ask other witnesses, such as a doctor or vocational expert, to come to the hearing. You and the witnesses answer questions under oath. The hearing is informal but is recorded. You and your representative, if you have one, may question witnesses and submit evidence.

After studying all the evidence, the Administrative Law Judge issues a written decision. The Administrative Law Judge sends you and your representative a copy of the decision or dismissal order.

Appeals Council Review

If you think the Administrative Law Judge's decision or dismissal order is wrong, you may ask the Appeals Council to review your case. The Appeals Council carefully examines your case and notifies you in writing of the action it takes.

The Appeals Council may grant, deny, or dismiss your request for review. If the Appeals Council grants your request, it will either decide your case or return it to the Administrative Law Judge for further action (which could include another hearing and a new decision). If the Council decides a formal review would not change the Administrative Law Judge's decision or dismissal, it will deny your request.

Federal Court Action

If you do not agree with the Appeals Council's decision or denial of your request for review of the Administrative Law Judge's decision, you may file a civil action in the United States District Court for the area where you live.

If you think any Administrative Law Judge treated you unfairly, you should tell Social Security Administration about it, and ask them to look into it even if you do not plan to file an appeal. The agency must receive your complaint within 180 days of either the date of the action, or the date you became aware of the conduct. You can file with the agency an unfair treatment complaint even while the agency is deciding your claim for benefits.

You should file your complaint in writing, or you can tell a Social Security agent about your complaint and they will write it down for you. Give as many details as you can, including:

- your name, address, and telephone number;
- your Social Security number;

- who treated you unfairly;
- how you think you were unfairly treated;
- when you think you were unfairly treated;
- the actions or words you thought were unfair; and
- who else saw or heard the unfair treatment.

A complaint should fully describe what the Administrative Law Judge did and said that you believe was unfair or inappropriate. Merely because you think that the Judge's decision was wrong, by itself, does not mean that the Judge was unfair or engaged in misconduct.

Note that filing an unfair treatment complaint is not the same as appealing a decision. If you received a decision on your claim, and you do not agree with it, you have 60 days from the date you receive the decision letter to ask for an appeal. The Judge's decision letter will explain how you should file an appeal. Although you can also describe the unfair treatment in your appeal, you should still file an unfair treatment complaint. If you believe that any Social Security employee or representative took an action that discriminated against you on the basis of race, religion, disability, language proficiency, age, sexual orientation, or gender identity, you may file a complaint. You may also file a complaint of program discrimination if you believe that Social Security policies, practices, or activities are discriminatory. You can ask for help at any Social Security office to make your complaint. You also can write to: Office of Hearings Operations, Division of Quality Service, Suites 1702/1703, 5107 Leesburg Pike, Falls Church, VA 22041–3255.

CHAPTER 13

EFFECT OF PENSIONS ON YOUR SOCIAL SECURITY BENEFITS

Although most people are covered by Social Security, and they will receive a stable income from these retirement benefits for as long as they live, the best situation for retirement planning and saving is to have a combination of retirement resources. In addition to your Social Security benefits, you would ideally want investments in IRAs, 401(k)s, annuities, life insurance, and a private pension from your employer. Your private pension can provide you with additional regular monthly income, while your other savings and investments can be used for unexpected expenditures and enjoyment.

Your Social Security retirement benefits will not be affected if you receive a private pension from employment for which you paid Social Security taxes. However, your Social Security benefits may be reduced if you get a retirement or disability pension from i) the federal civil service, ii) some state or local government employment, iii) work in a foreign country, or iv) any work not covered by Social Security.

You are among the fortunate if you have an aggregate of your private pension, your Social Security benefits, and your retirement funds. But the situations like yours are changing as many businesses have stopped providing their employees the traditional defined-benefits pension plans which pay a certain monthly amount for life. Instead, many employers now offer defined-contribution retirement plans where they will only contribute a certain amount each year to an employee's retirement plan. Even among public sector employers, the number of traditional defined-benefits pension plans have been reduced because of limited state and local government budgets. However, these defined-contribution plans, such as 401(k)s and the like, generally do not deliver a guaranteed monthly or yearly income stream to retirees.

If you receive a pension from a public sector employer your Social Security benefit payments may be reduced or eliminated depending on the circumstances. This is because rules and regulations such as the Windfall Elimination Provision and the Government Pension Offset can lessen the amount of benefit that you can get from Social Security.

Social Security Administration treats private pensions and public pensions differently because Social

Security is funded by payroll taxes collected from private employers and the self-employed. As discussed earlier, private sector employees pay 6.2 percent of their wages (up to a certain annual maximum) as a Social Security payroll tax which is matched by their private employers. These Social Security payroll taxes are used to make benefit payments to current Social Security retirees and others receiving benefits. In contrast, many public employees do not pay Social Security payroll taxes, and it was generally considered unfair that public employees should receive benefits they did not contribute to.

The net result of the distinction between private and public pensions is that Social Security benefits will be reduced for those who begin to receive public pensions. On the other hand, people who receive private pensions normally will experience no adverse impact on their Social Security benefit payments.

A likely situation where your public pension can adversely affect your Social Security benefits is if you split your career timeline between private and public employers. If you worked long enough in the private sector to earn 40 Social Security credits, you can claim Social Security retirement benefits based on your own work record. But, if you also qualify for a public pension, your Social Security benefits will be reduced when you start to collect your public pension. Another situation that will be adversely impacted by your receipt of a public pension is where you are receiving Social Security spousal or survivor benefits. In this case, your Social Security spousal or survivor benefits will be reduced if you get payments from your public pension.

One of the regulations that result in the reduction of your Social Security benefits is the Windfall Elimination Provision which can affect how Social Security Administration calculates your retirement or disability benefit. The Windfall Elimination Provision allows the Social Security Administration to reduce the amount of Social Security retirement benefits that you are eligible to receive if you worked both for a public employer and in the private sector at different stages of your career. If your public employment involved wages that were not subject to Social Security payroll taxes and also resulted in your earning a public pension, then the Windfall Elimination Provision prevents you from getting what is considered an unfair windfall.

If you work for an employer who does not withhold Social Security taxes from your salary, such as a government agency or an employer in another country, any retirement or disability pension you get from that work can reduce your Social Security benefits. This provision can affect you when you earn a retirement or disability pension from an employer who did not withhold Social Security taxes and you qualify for Social Security retirement or disability benefits from work in other jobs for which you did pay Social Security taxes.

The Windfall Elimination Provision can apply if, after year 1985:

- you reached 62;
- you became disabled; or
- you first became eligible for a monthly pension based on work where you did not pay Social Security taxes after 1985, even if you are still working.

The Windfall Elimination Provision also affects Social Security benefits for people who performed federal service under the Civil Service Retirement System (CSRS) after 1956. But Social Security Administration will not reduce your Social Security benefit payments if you only performed federal service under a system such as the Federal Employees' Retirement System (FERS) where Social Security taxes are withheld. Social Security Administration utilizes a formula to calculate benefits under the Windfall Elimination Provision.

The Windfall Elimination Provision does not apply to the following situations:

- you are a federal worker first hired after December 31, 1983;

- you are an employee of a nonprofit organization who was first hired after December 31, 1983;
- your only pension is for railroad employment;
- the only work you performed for which you did not pay Social Security taxes was before 1957; or
- you have 30 or more years of substantial earnings under Social Security.

Note that there are some protections that apply with the Windfall Elimination Provision. One protection is that the Social Security Administration has established a maximum reduction amount that applies depending on what year you turn 62 years old and how many years of substantial earnings in a Social Security–eligible job you had in your career. Another protection is that the Windfall Elimination Provision will never reduce your Social Security by more than half of the amount that you get from your public pension. To see the maximum amount that Social Security could reduce your benefits, visit www.social security.gov/planners/retire/wep-chart.html.

Another regulation called The Government Pension Offset allows the Social Security Administration to reduce what you get from Social Security in the form of spousal or survivor benefits if you also receive a public-sector pension payment. The Government Pension

Offset is focused on the benefits that you may be entitled to receive from Social Security based on the work record of someone else, instead of the retirement benefits available to you based on your own work record. The Government Pension Offset basically reduces your Social Security spousal or survivor benefits by two-thirds of the amount that you receive from your public pension. Thus, under this rule, there is no limit on the dollar amount that your Social Security spousal or survivor benefits can be reduced. This means that if you have a large public-sector pension compared to your spousal or survivor benefits, then the Government Pension Offset can reduce your Social Security spousal or survivor benefits to nothing.

Note that the Government Pension Offset covers only the Social Security spousal or survivor benefits that you receive. If you had a career in the private-sector and qualified for Social Security, and also receive a public pension, then you will still be entitled to your Social Security retirement benefits based on your own work record. The Government Pension Offset has no effect on your own Social Security retirement benefits. However, the Government Pension Offset could negatively affect you if your Social Security spousal or survivor benefit amount is bigger than your own Social Security retirement benefit.

The timing of when you start receiving your public pension and your Social Security benefits can be very important in optimizing your benefits. This is because the Windfall Elimination Provision and the Government Pension Offset are only applicable during the time when you are receiving both your public pension and your Social Security at the same time. This means that you can arrange the dates that you claim your public pensions and your Social Security retirement benefits such that you can minimize the effects of the Windfall Elimination Provision and the Government Pension Offset. For example, you can delay your Social Security benefits to increase the benefit amount as much as possible to absorb any impact of the Windfall Elimination Provision and the Government Pension Offset.

In some situations it may be better to delay your public pension and start Social Security benefits as early as possible. For example, if you will have a relatively large public pension which would reduce your Social Security spousal or survivor benefit to nothing, then it may make sense to start your Social Security benefits as soon as you can and wait to collect your public pension for as long as you can.

Government workers who are eligible for Social Security benefits on the earnings record of a spouse should read "Government Pension Offset" (Publication No. 05–10007) for more information. People who worked in another country, or government workers who are also eligible for their own Social Security benefits, read "Windfall Elimination Provision" (Publication No. 05–10045) for additional information.

CHAPTER 14

RECEIVING SOCIAL SECURITY BENEFITS OUTSIDE THE UNITED STATES

Your Social Security benefits will not be affected if you are a US citizen and travel to or live in most foreign countries. But, there are some countries where you cannot receive Social Security payments. Generally, Social Security Administration cannot send payments to the following countries:

- Azerbaijan,
- Belarus,
- Cuba,
- Kazakhstan,
- Kyrgyzstan,
- Moldova,
- North Korea,
- Tajikistan,
- Turkmenistan,

- Ukraine, and
- Uzbekistan.

However, some exceptions can be made for eligible beneficiaries in countries other than Cuba and North Korea. To qualify for an exception, you must meet and agree to restricted payment conditions. For more information about these conditions and the qualifications for an exception, contact the Social Security Administration or your Federal Benefits Unit. If you do not qualify for an exception, Social Security administration will withhold your payments until you leave the country with Social Security restrictions and go to a country where they can send payments.

If you are a US citizen residing in Cuba or North Korea, you can get all the payments that Social Security Administration has withheld once you move to a country where the agency can send payments. Under the Social Security Act, if you are not a US citizen, you cannot receive payments for the months you lived in Cuba or North Korea, even if you go to another country and satisfy all other requirements.

Social Security Administration applies different rules to determine if you can get benefit payments when you work outside the United States. You can get more information on this topic by reading "Your Payments While You Are Outside The United States" (Publication No. 05–10137) available from the agency and at www.socialsecurity.gov/pubs.

You can receive your Social Security payments outside the United States if you are a US citizen as long as you are eligible for benefits. You are considered outside the United States if you are not in one of the 50 states, the District of Columbia, the US Virgin Islands, Puerto Rico, Guam, the Northern Mariana Islands, or American Samoa. Social Security Administration will determine that you are outside the United States if you have been away from the above-mentioned territories for at least 30 days in a row. So, if you are traveling outside the United States for an extended period of time, then, you should let Social Security Administration know the date you plan to leave and the date you plan to return. The agency can then let you know if any of your Social Security benefits will be affected.

If you are not a US citizen, or you do not meet one of the conditions for continued payments, Social Security Administration will stop your payments after you have been outside the United States for 6 full calendar months. Once this happens, the agency cannot start your payments again until you come back and stay in the United States for a full calendar month. You must be in the United States on the first minute of the first day of any month and stay through the last minute of the last day of that month. In addition, you may have to prove you have been lawfully present in the United States for the full calendar month.

Social Security Administration provides a useful online tool (at www.socialsecurity.gov/international/ payments_outsideUS.html) which can help you find out if you can continue to receive your Social Security benefits if you are outside the United States, or you are planning to go outside the United States. This tool will help you find out if your retirement, disability, or survivor's payments will stop after 6 consecutive months or if certain country-specific restrictions apply.

Social Security Administration will periodically send you a questionnaire regarding your benefits and status if you live outside the United States. Be sure to return this questionnaire to the Social Security office which sent it to you, because it will be used to determine if you are still eligible for benefit payments. If you do not return this questionnaire, Social Security Administration will stop your benefit payments. You should also promptly notify the agency about any changes that you believe could affect your benefit payments.

Note that if you are a US citizen or a permanent resident of the United States (Green Card holder), you are subject to US income tax laws no matter where you live. This means that your worldwide income, including up to 85 percent of the Social Security benefits you get, may be subject to federal income tax.

If you are not a US citizen and want to receive Social Security payments while living outside the United States, you must i) qualify for benefits, ii) reside in a country where you can receive payments, and iii) meet one of these following conditions:

- you qualified for monthly Social Security benefits in December 1956, or the person on whose record your payments are based died or got a disability while in the US military service and was not dishonorably discharged;
- you qualify for benefits based on your earnings and are in active military service or had covered railroad employment;
- you were eligible for monthly Social Security benefits for December 1956; or
- the worker on whose record your benefits are based died while in the US military service or as a result of a service-connected disability, and was not dishonorably discharged.

If you are receiving benefits based on your own earnings and you meet one of the conditions below, Social Security Administration will continue your US Social Security payments.

- The worker on whose record your benefits are based had railroad work that the

Social Security program treated as covered employment; or
• You are in the active military or naval
service of the United States.
• However, if you are receiving your payments as a dependent or survivor, you must
also meet additional residency requirements for dependents and survivors which
are discussed later.

Social Security Administration will continue your
Social Security payments if you are a citizen of one
of the following countries in List 1 below:

List 1:
- Austria
- Belgium
- Canada
- Chile
- Czech
  Republic
- Finland
- France
- Germany
- Greece
- Hungary
- Ireland
- Israel
- Italy
- Japan
- Korea
  (South)
- Luxembourg
- Netherlands
- Norway
- Poland
- Portugal
- Slovak
  Republic
- Spain
- Sweden
- Switzerland
- United Kingdom

As this list of countries is subject to change, you should go to www.socialsecurity.gov/international/countrylist1.htm for the latest information.

If you are a citizen of one of the countries in List 2 below and you are receiving benefits based on your own earnings, Social Security Administration will continue your US Social Security benefit payments. Again, note that if you are receiving benefits as a dependent or survivor, you must also meet the additional residency requirements for dependents and survivors.

List 2:

- Albania
- Antigua and Barbuda
- Argentina
- Australia
- Bahama Islands
- Barbados
- Belize
- Bolivia
- Bosnia-Herzegovina
- Brazil
- Bulgaria
- Burkina Faso
- Colombia
- Costa Rica
- Côte d'Ivoire
- Croatia
- Cyprus
- Denmark
- Dominica
- Dominican Republic
- Ecuador
- El Salvador
- Gabon
- Grenada
- Guatemala
- Guyana
- Iceland
- Jamaica

- Jordan
- Latvia
- Liechtenstein
- Lithuania
- Macedonia
- Malta
- Marshall
  Islands
- Mexico
- Micronesia,
  Federal
  States of
- Monaco
- Montenegro
- Nicaragua
- Palau
- Panama
- Peru
- Philippines
- Romania

- Samoa
  (formerly
  Western
  Samoa)
- St. Kitts and
  Nevis
- St. Lucia
- St. Vincent
  and the
  Grenadines
- San Marino
- Serbia
- Slovak
  Republic
- Slovenia
- Trinidad-
  Tobago
- Turkey
- Uruguay
- Venezuela

This list of countries is subject to change and you should go to www.socialsecurity.gov/international/countrylist2.htm for the latest information.

If you are a resident of a country that has a US social security agreement (other than Austria, Belgium, Denmark, Germany, Sweden, or Switzerland), Social Security Administration will continue your US Social Security payments. Currently, the countries that have a social security agreement with the United States are included in List 3 below:

List 3:

- Australia
- Austria
- Belgium
- Canada
- Chile
- Czech Republic
- Denmark
- Finland
- France
- Germany
- Greece
- Hungary
- Ireland
- Italy
- Japan
- Luxembourg
- Netherlands
- Norway
- Poland
- Portugal
- Slovak Republic
- Spain
- South Korea
- Switzerland
- United Kingdom

Go to www.socialsecurity.gov/international/countrylist3 .htm for the latest information on this list of countries. If you are a resident (but not a citizen) of Austria, Belgium, Denmark, Germany, Sweden, or Switzerland, the social security agreements allow you to continue to receive your benefits only if you are:

- a refugee or stateless person; or
- receiving dependent or survivor benefits on the record of a worker who is (or was

at the time of death) a US citizen, a citizen of the country where you reside, a refugee, or stateless person.

Additional residency requirements for dependents and survivors apply. If you are a citizen of a country for which Social Security Administration requires dependents and survivors to meet additional residency requirements, you will have to show that you lived in the United States for at least 5 years. During those 5 years, you must have been in the family relationship on which your benefits are based.

However, the United States residency requirement does not apply if you meet any of the following conditions:

- you were initially eligible for monthly benefits before January 1, 1985;
- your entitlement is based on the record of a worker who died during US military service or as a result of a service-connected disease or injury;
- you are a citizen of a country included in List 3 on page 145; or
- you are a resident of a country (other than Austria, Belgium, Denmark, Germany, Sweden, or Switzerland) included in List 3 on page 145. Residency in Austria, Belgium, Denmark, Germany, Sweden, or

Switzerland means you, are subject to other conditions for Social Security payments to continue while you are outside the United States.

A child who has not lived in the United States for 5 years can meet the 5-year residency requirement if the parent who is the worker and the other parent have both lived in the United States for five years. However, the Social Security Administration will not pay children adopted outside the United States while they reside outside the United States, even if the child meets the residency requirement.

If you are a citizen of one of the countries listed in the List 4 below, Social Security Administration will continue to pay your benefits outside the United States if:

1. you are receiving benefits based on your own earnings, and you earned at least 40 credits under the US Social Security system or lived at least 10 years in the United States; or
2. you are receiving benefits as a dependent or survivor of a worker who earned at least 40 credits under the US Social Security system or lived in the United States for at least 10 years. You must also meet the additional residency requirements for dependents and survivors.

List 4:

- Afghanistan
- Bangladesh
- Bhutan
- Botswana
- Burma
- Burundi
- Cameroon
- Cabo Verde
- Central African Republic
- Chad
- China
- Congo, Republic of
- Eritrea
- Ethiopia
- Fiji
- Gambia
- Ghana
- Haiti
- Honduras
- India
- Indonesia
- Kenya
- Laos
- Lebanon
- Lesotho
- Liberia
- Madagascar
- Malawi
- Malaysia
- Mali
- Mauritania
- Mauritius
- Morocco
- Nepal
- Nigeria
- Pakistan
- Senegal
- Sierra Leone
- Singapore
- Solomon Islands
- Somalia
- South Africa
- Sri Lanka
- Sudan
- Swaziland
- Taiwan
- Tanzania
- Thailand
- Togo
- Tonga
- Tunisia
- Uganda
- Yemen

For the latest information on this list go to www. socialsecurity.gov/international/countrylist4.htm.

For more information about international social security agreements go to www.socialsecurity.gov /international/.

Social Security Administration applies the foreign work test and will withhold your Social Security benefits if you meet the following conditions:

a. you have not reached full retirement age; and
b. you work more than 45 hours a month outside the United States in employment or self-employment not subject to US Social Security taxes.

Your benefits will be withheld for each month that you fit those conditions. It does not matter how much you earned or how many hours you worked each day. Also, your benefits will be withheld if you are entitled to them as a dependent of someone whose benefits were withheld under the foreign work test. In this case, your benefits will be withheld for the same months as with the person that you are a dependent of, even if you are not working.

Under the foreign work test, Social Security Administration will determine you to be working any day that you:

• work as an employee or self-employed person;

- have an agreement to work even if you do not actually work because of sickness, vacation, etc.; or
- are the owner or part owner of a trade or business, even if you do not actually work in the trade or business, or do not make any income from it.

Your benefits are subject to the foreign work test if you are a US citizen or resident receiving US Social Security benefits, and you are working in a country that has an international social security agreement with the United States (see List 3 on page 145) which exempts your earnings from US Social Security taxes.

The annual retirement earnings test reduces your Social Security benefit payments if you are younger than full retirement age and continue to work. Under certain conditions, Social Security covers work by US citizens or residents outside the United States. If Social Security covers your work, the same annual retirement earnings test that applies to people in the United States applies to you. Under the annual retirement earnings test, you can still get all benefits due for the year if your earnings do not exceed the annual exempt amount. The exempt amount (which changes each year) for year 2020 is $18,240 if your full retirement age is after 2020. If the annual retirement earnings test applies to you, and your earnings exceed the annual exempt amount, Social Security

Administration will reduce some or all of your benefits by your earnings as follows:

- if you are younger than full retirement age, $1 in benefits will be reduced for each $2 in earnings above the limit.

If you are not a US citizen or do not meet one of the conditions for receiving payment abroad, the Social Security Administration will stop making payments to you after you have been abroad for six months. The payments will resume when you have stayed in the United States for one full month.

CHAPTER 15

BENEFITS UNDER THE SUPPLEMENTAL SECURITY INCOME PROGRAM

Supplemental Security Income (SSI) is Social Security Administration's safety net program for US citizens or nationals or certain aliens who are not able to meet their basic financial needs because of their age or a disability. If you get Social Security benefits, but have limited income and resources that you own, SSI may be able to help. SSI makes monthly payments to people who are age 65 or older or who are blind or disabled. Unlike Social Security, funding for SSI comes from the general US federal government revenues and not from Social Security taxes.

There are very specific requirements that you must meet to receive SSI benefits. In general these requirements are the following:

- you must file an application for SSI benefits;

- you must be 65 or older, or blind, or disabled;
- you must be a US citizen or national or a noncitizen who meets the alien eligibility criteria under the 1996 legislation and its amendments (generally, an alien who is subject to an active warrant for deportation or removal will not meet this citizenship/alien requirement);
- you must have limited income;
- you must have limited resources that you own;
- you must reside in one of the 50 US states, the District of Columbia or the Northern Mariana Islands;
- you must not be absent from the country for a full calendar month or for 30 consecutive days or more;
- you must not be confined to an institution (such as a hospital or prison) at the government's expense;
- you must apply for any other cash benefits or payments for which you may be eligible (for example, pensions, Social Security benefits); and
- you must give Social Security Administration permission to contact any financial

institution and request any financial records about you.

Note that Social Security Administration does count some of your income and some of your resources when it decides whether you are eligible for SSI. Also, in special cases, children under 18 may be considered disabled and eligible for SSI benefits. For a child to qualify, the disability must result in severe functional limitations and can be expected to cause death or has lasted (or is expected to last) longer than 12 months.

Income Limit for SSI:

The Federal Benefit Rate (FBR) outlines both the SSI income limit for eligibility and the maximum monthly SSI payment. The FBR currently sets monthly payments at $783 for an individual and $1,175 for couples, for the year 2020. The FBR will increase moderately each year in conjunction with the Social Security cost-of-living adjustment, which tracks inflation. The latest increase in January 2020 was 1.6 percent. An additional $392 per month may be paid for an essential person who is providing necessary basic care for the SSI recipient.

To become eligible for SSI, a person or couple's combined income cannot exceed the monthly SSI payment as outlined by the FBR. However, the Social Security Administration only counts portions of a person's income toward the income limit. For example, if you work and earn income, only half of the amount earned each month in excess of the first $65 will count when determining your eligibility for SSI. Because of the rules and requirements regarding SSI, you should always contact the Social Security Administration regarding your specific income and eligibility.

Forty-six of the states provide supplementary income which is added to the federal SSI payments. This additional money raises the allowed income level for SSI eligibility in these states. The supplemental amount will also increase the amount of the monthly SSI payment. The amount of the supplement varies from state to state, but it may be between $10 and $400 per month. No supplement is provided in Arizona, Mississippi, North Dakota, West Virginia, and the Northern Mariana Islands.

Blindness under SSI:

Here are the requirements to qualify for blindness under the SSI disability programs:

- you have a central visual acuity for distance of 20/200 or less in your better eye with use of a correcting lens; or
- you have a visual field limitation in your better eye, such that the widest diameter of the visual field subtends an angle no greater than 20 degrees.

If you are not blind according to the above requirements, but have a visual impairment, you may still be eligible for SSI benefits on the basis of disability.

Disabled under SSI:

If you are under age 18, you may be considered "disabled" under the SSI program if:

- you have a medically determinable physical or mental impairment (or combination of impairments); and
- the impairment(s) results in marked and severe functional limitations; and
- the impairment(s) has lasted (or is expected to last) for at least one year or to result in death.

To meet the definition of disability, the impairment(s) must result from anatomical, physiological, or psychological abnormalities that are demonstrable by medically acceptable clinical and laboratory diagnostic techniques.

You may be considered "disabled" under SSI if you are age 18 or older if you have a medically determinable physical or mental impairment (including an emotional or learning problem) which i) results in the inability to do any substantial gainful activity and ii) can be expected to result in death, or has lasted or can be expected to last for a continuous period of not less than 12 months.

Social Security Administration tries to provide benefits quickly to applicants whose medical conditions are so serious that their conditions clearly meet disability standards. Compassionate Allowances (CAL) are a way to quickly identify diseases and other medical conditions that, by definition, meet Social Security's standards for disability benefits. These conditions primarily include certain cancers, adult brain disorders, and a number of rare disorders that affect children. The CAL initiative helps reduce waiting time to reach a disability determination for individuals with the most serious disabilities.

Limited Income under SSI:
For the purposes of SSI, income includes:

- money you earn from work;
- money you receive from other sources, such as Social Security benefits, workers compensation, unemployment benefits, the Department of Veterans Affairs, friends or relatives; and
- any free food or shelter you receive.

Social Security Administration does not count all income for SSI, but income that it does count reduces your SSI benefit amount.

Some examples of payments or services that do not count as income for the SSI program are the following:

- the first $20 of most income received in a month;
- the first $65 of earnings and one-half of earnings over $65 received in a month;
- the value of Supplemental Nutrition Assistance Program (food stamps) received;
- income tax refunds;
- home energy assistance;
- assistance based on need funded by a State or local government, or an Indian tribe;
- small amounts of income received irregularly or infrequently;
- interest or dividends earned on countable resources or resources excluded under other Federal laws;
- grants, scholarships, fellowships or gifts used for tuition and educational expenses;
- food or shelter based on need provided by nonprofit agencies;
- loans to you (cash or in-kind) that you have to repay;

- money someone else spends to pay your expenses for items other than food or shelter (for example, someone pays your telephone or medical bills);
- income set aside under a Plan to Achieve Self-Support;
- earnings up to $1,870 per month to a maximum of $7,550 per year (effective January 2019) for a student under age 22;
- the cost of impairment-related work expenses for items or services that a disabled person needs in order to work;
- the cost of work expenses that a blind person incurs in order to work;
- disaster assistance;
- the first $2,000 of compensation received per calendar year for participating in certain clinical trials;
- refundable Federal and advanced tax credits received on or after January 1, 2010; and
- certain exclusions on Indian trust fund payments paid to American Indians who are members of a federally recognized tribe.

In calculating your SSI eligibility and benefit, Social Security Administration will subtract any income that they do not count from your total gross income to get the remaining amount which is your "countable income." Your countable income is then subtracted from the SSI Federal Benefit Rate to get your SSI Federal Benefit Amount as illustrated below.

1. Your Total Income minus Your income that we do not count = Your countable income
2. SSI Federal benefit rate minus Your countable income = Your SSI Federal benefit

There are situations Social Security Administration will deem you to have income. For example, if you are eligible for SSI benefits and live with your spouse who is not eligible for SSI benefits, some of your spouse's income may be counted in determining your SSI benefit. When a disabled or blind child under age 18 lives with parent(s), (or a parent and a step-parent), and at least one parent does not receive SSI benefits, some of the parents' income may be counted in figuring the child's SSI benefit. If an alien has a sponsor, with certain exceptions, some or all of the sponsor's income may be counted in figuring the SSI benefit. Any deemed income will not apply when you no longer live with a spouse or parent, when a disabled or blind child attains age 18, or when an alien's sponsorship ends.

Your living arrangement is another factor used to determine how much SSI benefits you can receive.

How much your SSI benefits are may vary depending on whether you live in your own place such as a house, apartment, or mobile home; or in someone else's household; or in a group home or care facility; or in an institution such as a hospital or a nursing home. Your SSI benefits could be reduced when you:

- live in another person's house, apartment, or mobile home, and you pay less than your fair share of your food or housing costs;
- live in your own house, apartment, or mobile home, and someone else pays for all or part of your food, rent, mortgage, or other things like electricity and heating fuel;
- are in a hospital or nursing home for the whole month and Medicaid pays for over one-half of the cost of your care; or
- are a minor child in a hospital or nursing home for the whole month and private insurance and/or Medicaid together pay over one-half your cost of care; or
- are in a public or private medical treatment facility and Medicaid is paying for more than half the cost of your care. If you are in the facility for the whole month, your

SSI benefit is limited to $30 (plus any sup-
plementary State payment). And your SSI
benefit may be reduced if you have other
income. However, you may be able to receive
your regular SSI benefit if you will be in a
medical institution for 90 days or less.

If you are homeless, your SSI benefit amount is calculated the same as for people who live in their own
houses, apartments, or mobile homes. And you can
live in a public shelter for up to 6 months out of any
9-month period and still receive up to the maximum
SSI benefit payment in your State.

Social Security Administration will count in-kind
support and maintenance as income when they figure the amount of your SSI benefits. In-kind support
and maintenance is food or shelter that somebody
else provides for you. This means that if someone
helps pay for your rent, mortgage, food, or utilities,
then the amount of your SSI benefits can be reduced.
If you receive any in-kind support and maintenance,
your monthly SSI benefits can be reduced as much as
$277, depending on the value of the help you receive.

Social Security Administration will not count
your in-kind support and maintenance in the following situations:

- you live only with your spouse and
  minor children and nobody outside the

household pays for your food and shelter; or

- you live with other people and pay your share of the food and shelter expenses.

Limited Resources under SSI:
Resources, for the purposes of SSI, are things you own such as: cash; bank accounts, stocks, US savings bonds, land; vehicles; personal property; life insurance; and anything else you own that could be converted to cash and used for food or shelter. Social Security Administration does not count the value of all of your resources for determining SSI eligibility. Here are the limits for resources which can be counted:

- Individual/Child—$2,000
- Couple—$3,000

Social Security Administration sometimes will deem a portion of the resources of a spouse, parent, parent's spouse, sponsor of an alien or sponsor's spouse as belonging to the person who applies for SSI. If a child who is under age 18 lives with one parent, $2,000 of the parent's total countable resources does not count. If the child lives with 2 parents, $3,000 does not count. Any amounts over the parents' limits are counted as part of the child's $2,000 resource limit.

Although the value of your resources is a factor in determining whether you are eligible for SSI benefits, keep in mind that not all of your resources count for SSI. If the value of your resources that count is over the allowable limit at the beginning of the month, you cannot receive SSI for that month. If you decide to sell the excess resources for what they are worth, you may receive SSI beginning the month after you sell the excess resources. You may also be able to receive benefits while you try to sell the excess resources in certain situations.

The following resources do not count in determining your eligibility for SSI benefits:

- the home you live in and the land it is on;
- household goods and personal effects (e.g., your wedding and engagement rings);
- burial spaces for you or your immediate family;
- burial funds for you and your spouse, each valued at $1,500 or less;
- life insurance policies with a combined face value of $1,500 or less;
- one vehicle, regardless of value, if it is used for transportation for you or a member of your household;
- retroactive SSI or Social Security benefits for up to nine months after

you receive them (including payments received in installments);

- grants, scholarships, fellowships, or gifts set aside to pay educational expenses for 9 months after receipt; and
- up to $100,000 of funds in an Achieving a Better Life Experience (ABLE) account established through a State ABLE program.

Other resources which do not count for SSI include these:

- property essential to self-support;
- resources that a blind or disabled person needs for an approved plan for achieving self-support;
- money saved in an Individual Development Account;
- support and maintenance assistance and home energy assistance that is not counted as income;
- cash received for medical or social services for a period of 1 month that is not counted as income;
- health flexible spending arrangements;
- State or local relocation assistance payments are not counted for 12 months;

- crime victim's assistance is not counted for 9 months;
- earned income tax credit payments are not counted for 9 months;
- dedicated accounts for disabled or blind children;
- disaster relief assistance which is not counted as income;
- cash received for the purpose of replacing an excluded resource (for example, a house) that is lost, damaged, or stolen is not counted for 9 months;
- federal tax refunds and advanced tax credits received on or after January 1, 2010 are not counted for 12 months;
- the first $2,000 of compensation received per calendar year for participating in certain clinical trials; and
- some qualified trusts.

If you are trying to sell real property or other resources that put you over the resource limit, you may be able to get conditional SSI benefits while you are trying to sell them. When you sell the resource, you must pay back the SSI benefits you received for the period in which you were trying to sell the property or other resource. You will be required to sign an "Agreement to Sell Property" form which must be accepted by Social Security Administration before conditional payments can begin. If you, your spouse, or a co-owner give away a resource or sell it for less than it is worth, you may be ineligible for SSI benefits for up to 36 months. How long you are ineligible for SSI benefits depends on the value of the resource you transferred.

Citizenship Status under SSI:

Beginning August 22, 1996, most non-US citizens must meet two requirements to be eligible for SSI. Non-US citizens must be in a qualified alien category and meet a condition that allows qualified aliens to get SSI benefits. Also, non-US citizens must meet all of the other requirements for SSI eligibility, including the limits on income, resources, and others.

There are seven categories of non-US citizens who are qualified aliens. You are a "qualified alien" if the Department of Homeland Security (DHS) designates you in one of these categories:

- lawfully admitted for Permanent Residence (LAPR) in the US, including "Amerasian immigrant" as defined in P.L. 100–202, with a class of admission AM-1 through AM-8;
- granted conditional entry under Section 203(a)(7) of the Immigration and Nationality Act (INA) as in effect before April 1, 1980;

- paroled into the United States under Section 212(d)(5) of the INA for a period of at least one year;
- refugee admitted to the United States under Section 207 of the INA;
- granted asylum under Section 208 of the INA;
- deportation is being withheld under Section 243(h) of the INA as in effect before April 1, 1997, or removal is being withheld under Section 241(b)(3) of the INA; or
- a "Cuban or Haitian entrant" under Section 501(e) of the Refugee Education Assistance Act of 1980 or in a status that is to be treated as a "Cuban/Haitian entrant" for SSI purposes.

Additionally, you can be a "deemed qualified alien" if, under certain circumstances, you, your child, or your parent has been subjected to battery or extreme cruelty by a family member while in the United States.

If you are in one of the 7 "qualified alien" categories listed above, or have been determined to be a "deemed qualified alien" because you have been subjected to battery or extreme cruelty, you may be eligible for SSI benefits if you have limited income and resources and are aged, blind, or disabled and also meet one of the following conditions:

- you were receiving SSI and lawfully residing in the United States on August 22, 1996; or
- you are a Lawfully Admitted for Permanent Residence (LAPR) with 40 qualifying quarters of earnings [Work done by your spouse or parent may also count toward the 40 quarters of earnings for getting SSI benefits. Social Security Administration will not count quarters of earnings toward the above requirements which are earned after December 31, 1996, if you, your spouse, or your parent(s) worked or received certain benefits from the US government based on limited income and resources during that period. If you entered the United States for the first time on or after August 22, 1996, then you may not be eligible for SSI for the first five years as a LAPR, even if you have 40 qualifying quarters of earnings.]; or
- you are currently on active duty in the US Armed Forces, or you are an honorably discharged veteran and your discharge is not because you are an alien. [This condition may also apply if you are the spouse, widow(er), or

dependent child of certain US military personnel.]; or

- you were lawfully residing in the United States on August 22, 1996, and you are blind or disabled.

You may receive SSI for a maximum of 7 years from the date you were granted qualified alien status in one of the following categories, and the status was granted within seven years of filing for SSI:

- refugee admitted to the United States (US) under section 207 of the Immigration and Nationality Act (INA);
- asylee admitted to the US under section 208 of the INA;
- alien whose deportation was withheld under section 243(h) of the INA or whose removal is withheld under section 241(b)(3) of the INA;
- admitted as a "Cuban or Haitian entrant"- as defined under section 501(e) of the Refugee Education Assistance Act of 1980 or in a status that is to be treated as a "Cuban/Haitian entrant" for SSI purposes; or
- "Amerasian immigrant" pursuant to P.L. 100–202, with a class admission of AM-1 through AM-8.

Certain categories of noncitizens may be eligible for SSI and are not subject to the August 22, 1996, law requirements. These categories include:

- American Indians born in Canada who were admitted to the United States under Section 289 of the INA; or
- noncitizen members of a Federally recognized Indian tribe who fall under Section 4(e) of the Indian Self-Determination and Education Assistance Act.

Additionally, you may be eligible for SSI under certain circumstances if the Department of Health and Human Services' Office of Refugee Resettlement and the Department of Homeland Security determine that you meet the requirements of the Trafficking Victims Protection Act of 2000. And, you may also qualify for SSI for a period of 7 years if you are an Iraqi or Afghani special immigrant admitted to the United States.

To meet the residency requirement for SSI, you must:

- live in the US, or the Northern Mariana Islands with the intent to continue living within the geographic limits; or
- be a child living with a parent in the military service assigned to permanent

duty ashore anywhere outside of the
United States; or

- be a student temporarily abroad for the
purpose of conducting studies as part
of an educational program.

Ineligibility for SSI:

There are some people who are not eligible for SSI
benefits. You are ineligible to receive SSI benefits
for any month during which you have an unsatisfied
felony or arrest warrant for: escape from custody; or
flight to avoid prosecution or confinement; or flight-
escape. Furthermore, Social Security Administration
cannot pay you any retroactive payments if you have
one of these unsatisfied felony or arrest warrants.
The agency will hold your retroactive payments until
you contact them and provide proof that you satisfied
the felony or arrest warrant.

If you are receiving SSI and you go to jail or
prison, then you are not eligible to receive SSI for
any full calendar month you are incarcerated. This
includes incarceration in correctional institutions,
detention centers, halfway houses, boot camps, and
the like, but might not include home confinement.
Furthermore, Social Security Administration can
not pay any retroactive payments for benefits due
before you were incarcerated. Any retroactive payments will be withheld until you contact the agency
and provide proof that you are no longer a prisoner.

In most instances, you can apply for SSI benefits several months before you expect to be released from prison or jail. For more information on how incarceration affects your SSI benefits, read Publication 10133 "What Prisoners Need to Know" at www.ssa. gov/pubs/10133.html.

If you are in any institution for a whole month that is run by a Federal, State or local government, you are not eligible for SSI for that month unless an exception applies such as residence in a public emergency shelter for the homeless or publicly operated community residence.

You may be ineligible for SSI for up to 36 months if you give away your resources or sell them for less than they are worth in order to reduce your resources below the SSI resource limit.

If you are receiving SSI as a noncitizen and you lose your status as an eligible alien, you are not eligible to receive SSI. For instance, your SSI benefits will stop if you lose your status as a qualified alien because there is an active warrant for your deportation or removal from the United States. If you are a qualified alien who no longer meets one of the conditions that allow SSI eligibility for qualified aliens, then your SSI benefits will stop.

You will not be eligible for SSI benefits for any month during all of which you have been outside the United States, with the exception of certain students temporarily abroad for study purposes or a child of military parents stationed overseas. And, after you have been outside the United States for 30 consecutive days or longer, you must be back in the United States for 30 consecutive days to be eligible for SSI benefits.

When an individual is eligible for past-due SSI benefits, Social Security must first reimburse the State if you received any monetary Interim Assistance, while you were waiting for your SSI decision. If the remaining past-due benefits are large, we must pay them in installments. The installment payments are made in no more than three payments, at six month intervals. There is an exception that allows the amount of the first and second payment to be increased because of certain debts. There are also two exceptions that would permit payment of all unpaid benefits due to you to be paid in one lump sum:

- if you have a medical condition that is expected to result in your death within 12 months; or
- you become ineligible for SSI benefits and are likely to remain ineligible for 12 months.

To apply for SSI, you can begin the process and sometimes complete most or all of your application online by visiting Social Security Administration's website at www.socialsecurity.gov/applyforbenefits.

You can also call toll-free at 1-800-772-1213 to set up an in-person or telephone appointment with a representative from your local Social Security office.

CHAPTER 16

BENEFITS UNDER THE MEDICARE PROGRAM

Medicare is the federal health insurance program for people age 65 or older, and for certain people with disabilities.

The Medicare program is run by the Health Care Financing Administration and Social Security Administration handles Medicare enrollment and provides general information.

Do not confuse Medicare with its companion program Medicaid. Medicaid, which is run by state social services, health or human services agencies and funded partially by the federal government, is a health insurance program for people with low income and limited assets. You may qualify for Medicare or Medicaid or both.

Medicare has these four parts:

- Medicare Part A (hospital insurance) helps pay for inpatient hospital care and certain follow-up services.
- Medicare Part B (medical insurance) helps pay for doctors' services, outpatient hospital care, and other medical services.
- Medicare Part C (Medicare Advantage plans) are private health insurance plans and are widely available. If you have Medicare Parts A and B, you can choose to receive all of your health care services through a private insurance company approved by Medicare to provide this coverage.
- Medicare Part D (Medicare prescription drug coverage) helps cover the cost of prescription drugs.

Eligibility and Coverage for Medicare Part A:
The vast majority of people get Medicare Part A when they turn 65. You automatically qualify for Part A if you are eligible for Social Security or Railroad Retirement Board benefits. You may also qualify based on your spouse's (including a divorced spouse's) work record. Further, you may qualify because you were a government employee not covered by Social Security, but who paid the Medicare tax.

If you get Social Security disability benefits for 24 months, you will qualify for Part A. You can also get Social Security disability benefits because you have amyotrophic lateral sclerosis (Lou Gehrig's disease), and you do not have to wait 24 months to qualify. And, if you have permanent kidney failure requiring dialysis or kidney replacement you would qualify for Part A if i) you worked long enough, or you are the spouse or child worker who qualifies.

If you do not meet these requirements, you may be able to get Medicare hospital insurance by paying a monthly premium. For more information, call Social Security Administration at their toll-free number or visit their website.

Certain people who were exposed to environmental health hazards are entitled to Part A and can enroll in Part B and Part D. These people have an asbestos-related disease and were present for at least six months in Lincoln County, Montana, 10 years or more before diagnosis.

Medicare Part A will help you cover the costs associated with all of the following types of care:

- inpatient care in a hospital;
- inpatient short-term care in a non-custodial skilled nursing facility;
- hospice care;
- home health care; and

- inpatient nonreligious and nonmedical items and services in a religious nonmedical health care institution (where the patient's religious beliefs prohibit conventional and unconventional medical care).

For inpatient hospital care, Medicare Part A covers semiprivate rooms, general nursing care, medicines as part of your inpatient treatment, meals, and other hospital supplies and services. It covers care that you receive in acute care, critical access, and long-term care hospitals; inpatient rehabilitation facilities; inpatient care associated with a qualifying clinical research study; and inpatient mental health care received in a psychiatric hospital or other hospital. For Medicare Part A-covered services you pay the prescribed copayments, coinsurance or deductibles for the services provided.

Note that Medicare Part A does not include:

- a private room unless medically necessary;
- any separate charges for a telephone or television; or
- personal care items, such as toothbrushes, razors or socks.

After a medically necessary stay at a hospital for at least 3 days, Medicare Part A will cover semiprivate rooms, meals, skilled nursing and rehabilitative services, and other required services and supplies in a skilled nursing facility. To qualify for skilled nursing facility coverage, your doctor has to certify that you need daily skilled care (such as physical therapy or intravenous injections) which can only be provided in an inpatient skilled nursing facility. Take notice that Medicare does not cover long-term or custodial care.

You can get Medicare coverage for hospice care if a hospice doctor and your doctor certify that you are terminally ill and have a life expectancy of 6 months or less. You must agree that you are receiving palliative care for comfort instead of other Medicare-covered treatments for your terminal illness. Hospice care is usually given in your home or other place where you are living, such as a nursing home. There are generally no costs to you for hospice care.

You can use your home health benefits under Medicare Part A and/or Part B home health-care services if you are house bound. This includes medically necessary part-time or intermittent skilled nursing care, physical therapy, speech-language pathology, occupational therapy services, medical social services, part-time home health aide services, durable medical equipment, and medical supplies for use at home. You pay nothing for covered home health services, but you pay 20 percent of the Medicare-approved amount and the deductibles for covered medical equipment.

For Medicare Part A-covered services in year 2020, you pay: $1,408 deductible for each benefit period. You pay no coinsurance for days 1–60 of covered inpatient care for each benefit period. But you pay $352 coinsurance per day for days 61–90 of covered inpatient or each benefit period. And you pay $704 coinsurance per each "lifetime reserve day" after day 90 for each benefit period (up to 60 days over your lifetime).You pay all costs for inpatient care beyond your lifetime reserve days.

Eligibility and Coverage for Medicare Part B:
Medicare Part B will help you with the costs of medically necessary doctor's services, outpatient care, home health services, durable medical equipment, mental health services, and other services (including many preventative services). Here is a list of some of the specific medical services covered by Medicare Part B:

- wellness and advance care planning;
- screening for abdominal aortic aneurysm, breast cancer, cardiovascular disease, cervical and vaginal cancers, colorectal cancer, diabetes, Hepatitis B, Hepatitis C, HIV, lung cancer, obesity, and prostate cancer;
- alcohol misuse and counseling;
- ambulance services to the nearest appropriate medical facility;

- chemotherapy;
- chiropractic services of the spine if medically necessary to correct subluxation;
- CPAP therapy if you have obstructive sleep apnea;
- diabetes treatment and supplies;
- home health services;
- kidney dialysis services and supplies;
- occupational and physical therapies;
- prosthetic and orthotic items; and
- transplants and immunosuppressive drugs.

Almost every person eligible for Part A can get Part B. But Part B coverage is optional and you usually pay a monthly premium. For example, in 2020, the standard monthly premium for Part B is $144.60. You will pay a higher Part B monthly premium if you have a higher income up to $491.60 if your adjusted gross income is $500,000 or more for a single tax filer. The year 2020 Part B deductible is $198 and the coinsurance is 20 percent of the Medicare-approved amount for the service.

Eligibility and Coverage for Medicare Part C:

Anyone who has Medicare Part A and Part B can join a Medicare Advantage plan. Medicare Advantage plans include:

- Medicare managed care plans;
- Medicare preferred provider organiza-
  tion (PPO) plans;
- Medicare private fee-for-service plans;
  and
- Medicare specialty plans.

In addition to your Medicare Part B premium, you might have to pay another monthly premium because of the extra benefits the Medicare Advantage plan offers.

Eligibility and Coverage for Medicare Part D:
Anyone with Medicare Part A or Medicare Part B is eligible for Medicare Part D prescription drug coverage. Medicare Part D is optional, and you pay an extra monthly premium for the coverage. The national base beneficiary premium for Part D coverage in year 2020 is $32.74 per month. Some people with higher incomes pay higher premiums because of a surcharge of $12.20 to $76.40 per month depending on income. Many people get their Part D coverage through a private Medicare Advantage plan.

Unless you are already getting Social Security benefits, you should contact Social Security Administration about three months before your 65th birthday to sign up for Medicare. You can and should sign up for Medicare even if you do not plan to retire at age 65.

If you are already receiving Social Security benefits or Railroad Retirement Board payments, Social
Security Administration will contact you a few
months before you become eligible for Medicare
and send you information. If you live in one of the
50 states, Washington, DC, the Northern Mariana
Islands, Guam, American Samoa, or the US Virgin
Islands, the agency will automatically enroll you in
Medicare Parts A and B. However, because you must
pay a premium for Part B coverage, you can choose
to reject it. Residents of Puerto Rico or foreign countries will not be enrolled in Part B automatically, but
they must elect Part B if they want it.

You will not be automatically enrolled in Medicare
Part D. You must elect Part D coverage because it is
optional and will require an extra premium. If you
do not enroll in Part B and Part D when you are
first eligible, you may have to pay a late enrollment
penalty for as long as you have Part B and Part D
coverage. Also, you may have to wait to enroll, which
will delay coverage.

For the latest information about Medicare, visit
the website or call the toll-free number listed below.

Medicare
Website: www.Medicare.gov
Toll-free number: 1-800-MEDICARE
(1-800-633-4227)

APPENDIX

Information in this Appendix is taken from various publications and other sources which are available free from the US Social Security Administration. This information is not intended as an endorsement or recommendation of this book, the author, or the publisher by US Social Security or any governmental agency.

A. Some Facts about Social Security
(Source: US Social Security Administration)

2020 Social Security taxes
- You pay 6.2 percent and your employer pays 6.2 percent.
- If you're self-employed, you pay 12.4 percent.
- You don't pay Social Security taxes on earnings greater than $137,700.

2020 Medicare taxes
- You and your employer each pay 1.45 percent.

- If you're self-employed, you pay 2.9 percent.
- Medicare taxes are paid on all of your earnings; there is no limit.
- There are additional Medicare taxes for higher-income workers.

Work credits in 2020

- For each $1,410 you earn, you receive one Social Security "credit," up to four per year.
- Most people need 40 credits to be eligible for retirement benefits.
- Younger people need fewer credits to qualify for disability benefits or for their family members to be eligible for survivors benefits.

Average estimated 2020 monthly Social Security benefits

- all retired workers: $1,499
- retired worker with an aged spouse: $2,511
- all disabled workers: $1,266
- disabled worker with a young spouse and one or more children: $2,185
- all aged widows and widowers: $1,422
- young widow or widower with two children: $2,951

Maximum Social Security retirement benefits for 2020

- Maximum retirement benefit a 65-year-old retiring in 2020 will receive is $2,857 per month.
- Maximum retirement benefit a 70-year-old retiring in 2020 will receive is $3,790 per month.

2020 monthly federal SSI maximum payment rates

(doesn't include state supplement, if any)

- $791 for an individual
- $1,187 for a couple

B. Frequently Asked Questions about Social Security
(Source: US Social Security Administration)

1. What's the best age to start receiving retirement benefits?

The answer is that there is not a "best" age that applies to everyone. It's a personal decision based on your situation and, ultimately, it is your choice. To help you make an informed choice, consider the factors below as you think about when to start receiving your Social Security benefits.

2. What does "retirement" mean?

For Social Security Administration, retiring means getting your Social Security retirement benefit. It might mean that you have also stopped working. However, these two things do not need to happen at the same time. For example, you have the option of delaying your monthly benefit even after you stop working. Delaying your benefit will increase your monthly benefit amount.

3. How are my Social Security Benefits calculated?

Your monthly benefit amount is based on your highest 35 years of earnings. If you do not have 35 years of earnings, your monthly benefit will be reduced, because years with no earnings will count as zeroes. Learn your estimated monthly benefit amount

by reading your Social Security Statement at www
.socialsecurity.gov/myaccount, or use the Retirement
Estimator at www.SocialSecurity.gov/retire/estimator
.html.

4. When should I start my Social Security retirement benefit?

You can start receiving benefits as early as age 62.
However, the longer you wait (up to age 70), the
higher your monthly benefit will be—for the rest of
your life. If you are married and you are the higher
earner, delaying your benefit may also mean higher survivor benefits for your spouse when you pass
away. You can see the impact of starting your monthly benefits at different ages by checking your Social
Security Statement or the Retirement Estimator.
Both are available online at www.socialsecurity.gov
/onlineservices. For more information on how delaying increases your monthly benefit, read the publication "When to Start Receiving Retirement Benefits"
(Publication No. 05- 10147), at www.socialsecurity
.gov/pubs/ EN-05-10147.pdf.

5. How is my "full retirement age" determined for
   Social Security benefits?

Your full retirement age for Social Security retirement
benefits is determined by the year you were born.
The retirement age used to be 65 for everyone, but
is gradually increasing to 67. As the full retirement

age goes up, benefits claimed at earlier ages go down. You can find out your full retirement age at www .socialsecurity.gov/planners/retire/ ageincrease.html.

6. Will my benefits be affected if I work while receiving Social Security benefits?

Working after you start receiving retirement benefits may affect your monthly benefit amount, depending on your age and how much you earn. If you are younger than your full retirement age, and your earnings exceed certain dollar amounts, some of your monthly benefit may be withheld. We will increase your monthly benefit <u>after you reach full retirement age</u> to account for the months of withheld benefits. When you reach your full retirement age, you can work and earn as much as you want and your benefit will not be affected. Find more information at www .socialsecurity.gov/planners/retire/whileworking.html.

Working can also increase your monthly benefit amount because benefits are based on your highest 35 years of earnings. If your current or future earnings are higher than one of the years we used to compute your retirement benefit, your benefit amount may increase slightly.

7. Can my Social Security benefit be taxed?

Some people have to pay federal income taxes on part of their Social Security benefits. This usually happens only if you have other substantial income (e.g., wages, interest, or dividends) in addition to your benefits. Learn more at www.socialsecurity.gov /planners/ taxes.html.

8. Am I eligible for spousal and family benefits under Social Security?
If you were married for 10 years or longer, you may be eligible for benefits on your ex-spouse's record. Do you have a spouse who is eligible based on your earnings record? Spouses and ex-spouses can generally receive up to half of the worker's full retirement age monthly benefit amount, and widow(er)s can receive more than that. However, if you are eligible for your own benefit and a spouse benefit, you will only receive the higher of the two benefit amounts. Learn more about benefits for your family at www.socialsecurity .gov/planners/ retire/applying7.html, spouse's benefits at www.socialsecurity.gov/planners/retire/ applying6 .html, and survivors benefits at www.socialsecurity .gov/planners/survivors.

9. Can I receive Social Security benefits if I am not a US citizen?
As long as you are legally present in the country and you and your employers have contributed to Social Security during your working years, you may be eligible for benefits. Social Security Administration's web page at www.socialsecurity.gov/planners/retire /applying5.html has more information.

10. Can my benefit be reduced if I worked in jobs not covered by Social Security?

If you worked in a job where you did not pay Social Security taxes, and you are now receiving a retirement or disability pension based on those earnings, your Social Security benefit may be affected. Learn more at www.socialsecurity.gov/planners/retire/gpo -wep.html.

11. Can I receive retroactive Social Security benefits?

If you are past your full retirement age when you start receiving benefits, you can choose to receive up to six months of retroactive monthly benefits. However, using this option changes the start of your benefit to an earlier date. Remember that by choosing to start your benefit earlier, your monthly benefit amount will be lower for the rest of your life, and your spouse's survivor benefits may also be lower.

12. When should I sign up for Medicare?

Consider whether you need to apply for Medicare at age 65, even if you are not applying for monthly retirement benefits. If you have already started receiving your retirement benefits, you will be automatically enrolled in Medicare when you turn 65. Medicare Part A (Hospital Insurance) is free for most people, and Medicare Part B (Medical Insurance) requires a monthly premium. Generally, if you have not already started receiving retirement benefits, you will want to sign up for Medicare three months before turning age 65, unless you have group health coverage through a current employer.

NOTE: If you do not have group health coverage through a current employer and you fail to sign up for Medicare Part B when you are first eligible, then you may have to pay a late enrollment penalty for as long as you have Part B. Also, you may have to wait to enroll, which will delay this coverage.

If you have a Health Savings Account (HSA) when you sign up for Medicare, you cannot contribute to your HSA once your Medicare coverage begins. If you contribute to your HSA after your Medicare coverage starts, you may have to pay a tax penalty. If you would like to continue contributing to your HSA, then you should not apply for Medicare, Social Security, or Railroad Retirement Board (RRB) benefits. Learn more at www.socialsecurity. gov/medicare or www.medicare.gov.

13. How can I get a Social Security Statement that shows a record of my earnings and an estimate of my future benefits?
You can get your personal Social Security Statement online by using your my Social Security account. If you do not yet have an account, you can easily create one. Your online Statement gives you secure and convenient access to your earnings records. It also shows estimates for retirement, disability and survivors

benefits you and your family may be eligible for. To set up or use your account to get your online Social Security Statement, go to https://secure.ssa.gov/RIL /SiView.action.

Social Security Administration also mails paper Statements to workers age 60 and older three months before their birthday if they do not receive Social Security benefits and do not yet have a my Social Security account.

14. How do I apply for my Social Security Benefits? Once you have decided on the date that you want to start receiving your monthly Social Security benefit, you can apply up to four months before the date you want your benefits to start. Visit www.socialsecurity. gov/retire to apply.

For more information, read Social Security Administration's publication, "When to Start Receiving Retirement Benefits" (Publication No. 05–10147), at www.socialsecurity.gov/pubs/EN-05 -10147.pdf, and visit the Retirement Planner at www .socialsecurity.gov/planners/retire.

C. Setting Up and Using an Online Social Security Account

(Source: US Social Security Administration)

It is easy for you to set up a secure online "my Social Security" account. Your my Social Security account can be your online gateway to Social Security Administration. It provides interactive, customizable, and secure access to many Social Security online services. Creating an account gives you the control to check your Social Security Statement, change your address, verify your reported earnings, estimate your future benefits, and much more.

Here is what you can do in your my Social Security account if you are not currently receiving Social Security benefits:

- compare retirement benefit estimates based on your selected date or age to begin receiving benefits with retirement estimates for ages 62, Full Retirement Age (FRA), and 70 with the new Retirement Calculator;
- request a replacement Social Security card if you meet certain requirements;
- check the status of your application or appeal;
- get your Social Security Statement;
- view estimates of your future benefits;

- verify your earnings;
- view the estimated Social Security and Medicare taxes you have paid; and
- get a benefit verification letter.

If you are currently receiving Social Security benefits, here are the many things that you can do online in your my Social Security account:

- request a replacement Social Security card if you meet certain requirements;
- report your wages if you work and receive Social Security Disability Insurance (SSDI) and/or Supplemental Security Income (SSI) benefits;
- get your benefit verification letter;
- check your benefit and payment information;
- change your address and phone number;
- start or change direct deposit of your benefit payment;
- request a replacement Medicare card;
- get a replacement SSA-1099 or SSA-1042S for tax season; and
- opt out of receiving mailed notices for those available online.

If you are a Representative Payee, here are the things that you can handle in your my Social Security account:

- use the Representative Payee Portal to conduct your own business or manage direct deposits, wage reporting, and annual reporting for your beneficiaries;
- complete and submit Representative Payee Accounting Reports;
- see the status of any completed Representative Payee Accounting Report; and
- receive a receipt for any report you submit.

You can create a my Social Security account if you are age 18 or older, have a Social Security number, a valid US mailing address, and an email address. To create an account, go to www.socialsecurity.gov /myaccount.

You will need to provide some personal information to confirm your identity. You will be requested to choose a username and password, and then you will be asked for your email address. You will have to select how you would like to receive a one-time security code—to a text3 enabled cell phone or to the email address you registered. You will need to enter this code to finish creating your account. Each time you sign in with your username and password, we will send a security code to your cell phone or to your email address. The security code is part of Social Security Administration's enhanced security feature to protect your personal information. Note that your cell phone provider's text message and data rates may apply.

GET PERSONALIZED RETIREMENT BENEFIT ESTIMATES

You can use Social Security Administration's online Retirement Estimator to get immediate and personalized retirement benefit estimates to help you plan for your retirement. The online Retirement Estimator is a convenient and secure financial planning tool that eliminates the need to manually key in years of earnings information. The estimator will also let you create "what if" scenarios.

You can, for example, change your "stop work" dates or expected future earnings to create and compare different retirement options. For more information, read the publication "Online Retirement Estimator" (Publication No. 05–10510), or visit the website at www.socialsecurity.gov/estimator.

D. Identity Theft and Fraud
(Source: US Social Security Administration)

IDENTITY THEFT

Every year, millions of Americans become victims of identity theft. Identity theft occurs when someone steals your personally identifiable information and pretends to be you. They can use this information to open bank or credit card accounts, file taxes, or make new purchases in your name. It is important that you take steps to protect your Social Security number from theft.

Be careful with your Social Security card and number to prevent identity theft. To minimize the risk of identity theft, keep your Social Security card and any other documents that show your Social Security number in a safe place. Do not carry your Social Security card or other documents with you that display your number unless you need them.

If someone obtains your Social Security number, they can use it to get other personal information about you, including your bank or credit information. Someone can steal your Social Security number by:

- stealing wallets, purses, and your mail (bank and credit card statements, pre-approved credit offers, new checks, and tax information);

- stealing personal information you provide to an unsecured site online, from business or personnel records at work, and personal information in your home;
- rummaging through your trash, the trash of businesses, and public trash dumps for personal data;
- posing by phone or email as someone who legitimately needs information about you, such as employers or landlords; or
- buying personal information from "inside" sources. (For example, an identity thief may pay a store employee for information about you that appears on an application for goods, services, or credit.)

If someone asks for your number, you should ask why, how it will be used, and what will happen if you refuse. But, make sure you give your employer and your financial institution(s) your correct Social Security number, so your records and tax information are accurate.

If you suspect that someone is using your Social Security number for work purposes, report the problem immediately by contacting the Federal Trade Commission. Social Security Administration will review your earnings with you to ensure its records are accurate. You may also verify your earnings on your Social Security Statement. You can get your Statement online by opening a personal my Social Security account.

If someone misused your Social Security number to create credit or other problems for you, immediately go to http://www.identitytheft.gov and report the identity theft to the Federal Trade Commission. Their website provides detailed information to help you defend against identity theft. You can reach them by phone by calling 1-877-IDTHEFT (1-877-438-4338); TTY 1-866-653-4261.

You may also want to contact the Internal Revenue Service (IRS), and file an online complaint with the Internet Crime Complaint Center at www.ic3.gov. Safeguarding your identity and Social Security is of the utmost importance. If you think you are a victim of identity theft, please act now.

During tax season, scammers are out in full force. Perhaps you received a phone call demanding payment from the IRS. They may threaten you with legal action if you do not pay immediately, or say things like, "we are sending the police to arrest you." While these calls may seem scary, it is important to understand that they are not legitimate. This scam, which started in October 2013, has claimed over $29 million from its victims. Unfortunately, this is just one of many scams designed to make you believe you are speaking with a legitimate government official.

Scammers use many tactics in an attempt to force victims to give out information, and sometimes money, via telephone or email. In Social Security–related scams, they often call under a guise of helping you complete a disability application, asking you for your Social Security number or banking information.

Whether they are with Social Security or the IRS, a government employee will never do some things as part of official agency business, including:

- call you to demand an immediate payment;
- demand that you pay a debt without the ability to appeal the amount you owe;
- require a specific means of payment, such as requiring you to pay with a prepaid debit card;
- ask you for your personal information or credit or debit card numbers over the phone; or
- threaten you with arrest or deportation.

Any legitimate request from a government agency will come to you in writing. Additionally, if you do receive a call from a government official, they will be able to provide you with a telephone number and extension. If you are attempting to conduct business with any government agency, or you have received a notice from such an agency, please utilize the telephone numbers provided in the notification. Additionally, you can find contact information on any .gov website such as socialsecurity.gov or irs.gov.

If you receive one of these scam calls or emails, do not provide them with any information. You should:

- hang up immediately;
- for Social Security impersonations, contact Social Security's Office of Inspector General at https://oig.ssa.gov/report;
- for IRS impersonations, contact the US Treasury Inspector General for Tax Administration (TIGTA) at www.treasury.gov/tigta, using the "IRS Impersonation Scam Reporting" page; and
- contact the Federal Trade Commission on FTC.gov.

Social Security Administration is committed to protecting the information and resources entrusted to it, including your personal information and investment. However, scam artists might try to trick you into sharing your personal information or money. Social Security Administration is there to help you identify and report these kinds of schemes.

The Office of the Inspector General (OIG) has a new web page with tips on how to protect yourself from theft, schemes, how to report scams, and recent fraud advisories. This is in response to an ongoing phone scheme, where individuals receive a call with a recorded message claiming to be from the OIG. The message states the individual's Social Security account, Social Security number, and/or benefits are suspended, and that they should call a non-Social Security phone number (which is not associated with Social Security Administration) to resolve the issue. When the individual calls this number, an unknown person pressures them into providing money or gift cards to resolve a fabricated issue, such as a warrant for the individual's arrest.

Social Security does not solicit your personal information over the phone or by email, or request advance fees for services in the form of wire transfers or gift cards. If anyone pressures you to provide personal information or money over the phone, just hang up.

FRAUDULENT AND MISLEADING ADVERTISEMENTS

Consumers nationwide are often misled by advertisers who use "Social Security" or "Medicare" to entice their victims. Often, these companies offer Social Security services for a fee, even though the same services are available directly from Social Security free of charge.

These services include matters such as getting:

- a corrected Social Security card showing a bride's married name;
- a Social Security card to replace a lost card;
- a Social Security Statement; and
- a Social Security number for a child.

Some fraudulent direct marketers suggest that Social Security is in dire financial shape and that people risk losing their Social Security or Medicare benefits unless they send a contribution or membership fee to the marketer. Other companies give the false impression of a Social Security endorsement or affiliation by offering a "Social Security Update" or related benefit update. Typically, these companies solicit information from consumers and then resell the consumer's private information. These marketing practices clearly mislead and deceive the American public.

Social Security Administration is very active in combatting misleading advertising using federal laws such as Section 1140 of the Social Security Act. Section 1140 is a consumer-protection tool against misleading advertising that prohibits the use of Social Security's words and symbols in a manner that conveys the false impression that Social Security issued or approved the communication. Section 1140 prohibits individuals and companies from:

- Misleading consumers by giving a false impression that Social Security Administration is associated with or endorses the communication. (Prohibited communications can take many forms, including mailed, emailed, and televised advertisements, websites, social media, personally targeted advertisements, mobile applications, and text messages.); and
- Reproducing and selling Social Security publications without authorization, as well as charging for services without notice that Social Security provides them for free.

Social Security's Office of the Inspector General (OIG) can impose civil monetary penalties, using authority delegated from the Commissioner of Social Security, against individuals, organizations, and other entities that violate Section 1140. If you receive misleading information about Social Security, then send the ad or information to:

Office of the Inspector General Fraud Hotline
Social Security Administration
PO Box 17768
Baltimore, MD 21235

Also, advise your state's attorney general or consumer affairs office and the Better Business Bureau in your area.

If you receive misleading information about Medicare, then you should contact the Office of Inspector General for the Department of Health and Human Services at the following address:

US Department of Health & Human Services
Office of Inspector General
Attn: HHS Tips Hotline
PO Box 23489
Washington, DC 20026

FRAUD

The risk of fraud in a far-reaching, complex system like Social Security is always present. Social Security provides benefits to about one-fifth of the American population and serves as a vital protection for working men and women, children, people with disabilities, and the elderly. The agency will pay approximately one trillion dollars in Social Security benefits to roughly 65 million individuals in 2020. Almost eight million people will receive Supplemental Security Income (SSI), on average, each month during 2020.

Beyond those who receive Social Security benefits, about 178 million people will pay Social Security taxes in 2020 and will benefit from the program in the future. That means nearly every American has an interest in Social Security, and Social Security Administration is committed to protecting their investment in these vital programs. Because the agency's benefit programs are so far-reaching, the agency faces the ongoing challenge of protecting the programs from fraud. To meet this challenge, the agency works closely with our Office of the Inspector General (OIG), which Congress has designated the agency lead for fraud detection and prevention.

Social Security Administration aggressively investigates allegations of fraud and is steadfast in its pursuit and prosecution of people who commit fraud. The message from the agency to those who attempt to defraud Social Security is clear: "We will find you; we will prosecute you; we will seek the maximum punishment under the law; and we will fight to restore the money you have stolen from the American people."

Moreover, Social Security Administration will continue pursuing additional anti-fraud initiatives, because the agency has zero tolerance for fraud and believes that any level of fraud is unacceptable.

The OIG works closely with Social Security Administration's frontline employees to identify fraud, root out offenders, and bring them to justice. In close coordination with the OIG, the agency uses a variety of proven techniques that identify fraud and help investigators analyze suspicious or question-able claims. They have been successful at combating fraud by using data analytics, collaborating with various agencies to pool investigative resources, and employing technology to prevent fraud. Some of Social Security Administration's anti-fraud initiatives include the following:

- The Cooperative Disability Investigations (CDI) program is one of Social Security's most successful anti-fraud initiatives. CDI units bring together personnel from Social Security, OIG, state disability determination services (DDS), and state and local law enforcement agencies to investigate suspicious or questionable Social Security disability claims. Currently, they have 46 units covering 40 states, the District of Columbia, the Commonwealth of Puerto Rico and the territories of American Samoa, Guam, the Northern Mariana Islands, and the US Virgin Islands. The efforts of the CDI units help ensure payment accuracy, generate significant taxpayer savings, and recover fraud losses for both federal and state programs.
- Social Security fraud prosecutors work with offices of the US Attorney around the country to bring federal

criminal charges against individuals who defraud Social Security programs. These prosecutors obtain criminal sanctions to include imprisonment, and funds recovery for the agency through criminal restitution and forfeiture.

- In addition to criminal charges and restitution, federal law (Section 1129 of the Social Security Act) gives Social Security Administration the authority to impose a civil monetary penalty against people who defraud Social Security. When the OIG's investigators find evidence that someone provided false information or withheld information that could affect eligibility for benefits, they can impose a civil monetary penalty of up to nearly $8,500 for each occurrence and an assessment in lieu of damages of up to double the amount of benefits paid as a result of the fraud. They may also impose a civil monetary penalty and assessment against representative payees or joint bank account holders who misuse payments.
- Social Security Administration is also authorized to impose administrative sanctions (Section 1129A of

the Social Security Act), when a person knowingly provides false or misleading information to the agency or fails to report information relevant to eligibility or benefit amount. Note that during a sanction period, Social Security benefits stop to the persons being sanctioned. The sanction periods are 6 months for the first occurrence, 12 months for the second occurrence, and 24 months for each additional occurrence.

- Social Security's Office of Anti-Fraud Programs (OAFP) and fraud prevention units identify potential fraud and prevent fraud at the earliest possible point in the decision-making process.
- One of the leading reasons people receive SSI payments for which they are not due is because they fail to properly notify Social Security Administration that they have more money in their financial accounts than allowed while collecting payments. The Access to Financial Institutions (AFI) program allows the agency to identify undisclosed financial accounts that have large amounts of money that would preclude the individual from receiving SSI

212

payments. Learn more about AFI at www
.ssa.gov/improperpayments/afi.html.

Not all improper payments occur due to fraud. That does not mean Social Security Administration will not try to recover those payments or prevent them from happening. The agency has a number of safeguards in place to ensure it pays people the right benefit amount at the right time. For example, the agency periodically reviews cases of those receiving disability benefits to ensure they are still eligible to receive them. The agency conducts a continuing disability review on each person receiving disability benefits approximately every three to seven years.

For people receiving SSI payments, the agency regularly reviews a person's income, resources, and living arrangements to make sure they still meet the eligibility requirements. The agency conducts a redetermination on most SSI recipients about once every one to six years. When it finds that a person has been paid money that they should not have received, it works to collect any amount of benefits paid incorrectly. If the person continues to receive benefits, the agency withholds a portion of the person's monthly payment until the debt, or overpayment, is paid.

In addition to these safeguards, Social Security Administration regularly conducts quality assurance and performance reviews to make sure decisions and payments are correct for people applying for and receiving benefits. You can join Social Security Administration in protecting your investment by reporting scams, fraud, waste, and abuse.

For more information on Social Security Administration's anti-fraud efforts, and to find a more comprehensive list of the tools and initiatives it uses to combat fraud, visit www.socialsecurity.gov /antifraudfacts.

E. RETIREMENT RESOURCES

Benefit Eligibility Screening Tool (BEST) at https://ssabest.benefits.gov/ helps to identify Social Security programs for which you may be eligible.

"Planning for Retirement/Retiring" at https://www.mymoney.gov/Fast/Pages/Results.aspx?k=Retirement%20OR%20Retiring&r=lifeevent provides links to a variety of retirement planning tools.

The Employee Benefit Research Institute, Ballpark E$timator at https://www.ssa.gov/agency/disclaimer.html?link=http%3A%2F%2Fwww.choosetosave.org%2Fballpark%2F is a useful calculator to get a basic idea of how much you need to save before you retire.

The site at https://www.usa.gov/retirement provides a variety of financial planning tools, including a Federal Employees Retirement Calculator.

F. HOW TO CONTACT SOCIAL SECURITY
(Source: US Social Security Administration)

There are several ways to contact Social Security, including online, by phone, and in person. They are there to answer your questions and to serve you. For more than 80 years, Social Security has helped secure today and tomorrow by providing benefits and financial protection for millions of people throughout their life's journey.

The most convenient way to conduct Social Security business from anywhere, at any time, is to visit www.socialsecurity.gov. There, you can:

- create a my Social Security account to review your Social Security Statement, verify your earnings, print a benefit verification letter, change your direct deposit information, request a replacement Medicare card, get a replacement SSA-1099/1042S, and more;
- apply for Extra Help with Medicare prescription drug plan costs;
- apply for retirement, disability, and Medicare benefits;
- find copies of Social Security Administration publications; and
- get answers to frequently asked questions and more.

Social Security Administration offers many automated services by telephone, 24 hours a day, 7 days a week. Call toll-free at 1-800-772-1213 or, if you are deaf or hard of hearing, at the TTY number 1-800-325-0778.

If you need to speak to a person, you can call from 7 a.m. to 7 p.m., Monday through Friday. Patience may be required during busy periods since you may experience a higher than usual rate of busy signals and longer hold times to speak to someone.

If you are in the United States, the British Virgin Islands, Canada, or Samoa, you may visit the nearest Social Security office to meet directly with a Social Security Administration representative. To find the nearest office, use the Social Security Office Locator at www.socialsecurity.gov/locator.

Foreign Country Service Information
If you are outside the United States, you have access to Social Security services at a number of Social Security Field Offices and American embassies and consulates who have specially trained personnel to assist you. Here is a list of US Embassies and Consulates around the world (also available at http://www.usembassy.gov/) that can help you with your Social Security matters.

LIST OF US EMBASSIES AND CONSULATES PROVIDING SOCIAL SECURITY ASSISTANCE

Afghanistan Federal Benefits Unit United States Embassy Via Veneto 119 / A 00187 Rome Italy Inquiries/Contact: https: //it.usembassy.gov/u-s -citizen-services/fbu/ fbu-rome-inquiry-form/ Fax: 39-06-4674-2542	**Albania** Federal Benefits Unit United States Embassy Via Veneto 119 / A 00187 Rome Italy Inquiries/Contact: https: //it.usembassy.gov/u-s -citizen-services/fbu/ fbu-rome-inquiry-form/ Fax: 39-06-4674-2542	**Algeria** Federal Benefits Unit United States Embassy 4 Avenue Gabriel 75382 Paris Cedex 08 France Phone: 331-4312-2705 Fax: 331-4312-2623 Email: FBU.Paris@ssa.gov
Andorra Federal Benefits Unit United States Embassy Serrano 75 28006 Madrid Spain Phone: 349-1587-2261 Fax: 349-1587-2260 Email: FBU.Madrid@ssa .gov	**Angola** Federal Benefits Unit United States Embassy Avenida das Forcas Armadas 1600 Lisbon Portugal Phone: 351-2172-73300 Fax: 351-2172-68696 Email: FBU.Lisbon@ssa.gov	**Anguilla** Federal Benefits Unit United States Embassy Av. Republica de Colombia # 57 Santo Domingo Dominican Republic Phone: 809-368-7011 Fax: 809-368-7854 Email: FBU.Santo. Domingo@ssa.gov
Antigua & Barbuda Federal Benefits Unit United States Embassy Av. Republica de Colombia # 57 Santo Domingo Dominican Republic Phone: 809-368-7011 Fax: 809-368-7854 Email: FBU.Santo. Domingo@ssa.gov	**Argentina** Federal Benefits Unit United States Embassy 4300 Colombia 1425 Buenos Aires Argentina Phone: 5411-5777-4492 Fax: 5411-5777-4231 Email: FBU.Argentina@ ssa.gov	

Bahamas
Federal Benefits Unit
United States Embassy
Av. Republica de Colombia
#57
Santo Domingo
Dominican Republic
Phone: 809-368-7011
Fax: 809-368-7854
Email: FBU.Santo.
  Domingo@ssa.gov
	Bahrain
	Federal Benefits Unit
	United States Embassy
	Via Veneto 119/A
	00187 Rome
	Italy
	Inquiries/Contact: https://
	  it.usembassy.gov/u-s-
	  citizen-services/fbu/
	  fbu-rome-inquiry-form/
	Fax: 39-06-4674-2542
		Bangladesh
		Federal Benefits Unit
		United States Embassy
		1201 Roxas Boulevard
		Ermita, Manila 0930
		Philippines
		Phone: 632-5301-2000
		Fax: 632-8708-9714
		  or 632-8708-9723
		Email: FBU.Manila@ssa
		  .gov
			Barbados
			Federal Benefits Unit
			United States Embassy
			Av. Republica de Colombia
			#57
			Santo Domingo
			Dominican Republic
			Phone: 809-368-7011
			Fax: 809-368-7854
			Email: FBU.Santo.
			  Domingo@ssa.gov

Belarus
Federal Benefits Unit
United States Embassy
ul. Piekna 12
00-539 Warsaw
Poland
Fax: 48-22-504-2281
Email: FBU.Warsaw@ssa
  .gov
	Belgium
	Federal Benefits Unit
	United States Embassy
	42 Elgin Road
	Ballsbridge
	Dublin 4
	Ireland
	Phone: 353-1668-8777
	  Ext: 2112
	(Mornings Only)
	Fax: 353-1668-7245
	Email: FBU.Dublin@ssa.gov
		Belize
		Federal Benefits Unit
		United States Embassy
		Calle 120 Avenida 0
		Pavas 1200
		San Jose
		Costa Rica
		Phone: 506-2519-2228
		Fax: 506-2291-1032
		Email: FBU.CostaRica
		  @ssa.gov
			Benin
			Federal Benefits Unit
			United States Embassy
			4 Avenue Gabriel
			75382 Paris Cedex 08
			France
			Phone: 331-4312-2705
			Fax: 331-4312-2623
			Email: FBU.Paris@ssa.gov

Bermuda	Bhutan	Bolivia	Bonaire
Federal Benefits Unit United States Embassy Av. Republica de Colombia # 57 Santo Domingo Dominican Republic Phone: 809-368-7011 Fax: 809-368-7854 Email: FBU.Santo. Domingo@ssa.gov	Federal Benefits Unit United States Embassy 1201 Roxas Boulevard Ermita, Manila 0930 Philippines Phone: 632-5301-2000 Fax: 632-8708-9714 or 632-8708-9723 Email: FBU.Manila@ssa .gov	Federal Benefits Unit United States Embassy Calle 120 Avenida 0 Pavas 1200 San Jose Costa Rica Phone: 506-2519-2228 Fax: 506-2291-1032 Email: FBU.CostaRica @ssa.gov	Federal Benefits Unit United States Embassy Av. Republica de Colombia # 57 Santo Domingo Dominican Republic Phone: 809-368-7011 Fax: 809-368-7854 Email: FBU.Santo. Domingo@ssa.gov

Bosnia Herzegovina	Botswana	Brazil	British Virgin Islands
Federal Benefits Unit	Federal Benefits Unit	Federal Benefits Unit	The office below that is
United States Embassy	United States Embassy	United States Embassy	nearest to you:
91 Vasilisis Sophias Avenue	33 Nine Elms Lane	Avenida das Forcas	SSA Field Office
101 60 Athens	London	Armadas	Professional Building
Greece	Sw11 7US	1600 Lisbon	4500 Sion Farm
Phone: 302-1072-02426 or	Phone: 44-207-499-9000	Portugal	Centerline Road
302-1072-02412	(8:30 – 1:00)	Phone: 351-2172-73300	Christiansted
Fax: 302-1064-69885	Fax: 44-207-891-3631	Fax: 351-2172-68696	US Virgin Islands 00820
Email: FBU.Athens@ssa.gov	Email: FBU.London@ssa.gov	Email: FBU.Lisbon@ssa.gov	Phone: 809-778-5946
			Fax: 809-778-2116
			SSA Field Office
			1st Floor – Nisky Center
			Nisky Shopping Center
			Charlotte Amalie
			US Virgin Islands
			Phone: 809-714-0136
			Fax: 809-714-1647
			Email: FBU.Santo.
			Domingo@ssa.gov

Brunei	**Bulgaria**	**Burkina Faso**	**Burma** (Myanmar)
Federal Benefits Unit	Federal Benefits Unit	Federal Benefits Unit	Federal Benefits Unit
United States Embassy	United States Embassy	United States Embassy	United States Embassy
1201 Roxas Boulevard	91 Vasilisis Sophias Avenue	4 Avenue Gabriel	1201 Roxas Boulevard
Ermita, Manila 0930	101 60 Athens	75382 Paris Cedex 08	Ermita, Manila 0930
Philippines	Greece	France	Philippines
Phone: 632-5301-2000	Phone: 302-1072-02426 or	Phone: 331-4312-2705	Phone: 632-5301-2000
Fax: 632-8708-9714 or	302-1072-02412	Fax: 331-4312-2623	Fax: 632-8708-9714 or
632-8708-9723	Fax: 302-1064-69885	Email: FBU.Paris@ssa.gov	632-8708-9723
Email: FBU.Manila@ssa.gov	Email: FBU.Athens@ssa.gov		Email: FBU.Manila@ssa.gov
Burundi			
Federal Benefits Unit			
United States Embassy			
4 Avenue Gabriel			
75382 Paris Cedex 08			
France			
Phone: 331-4312-2705			
Fax: 331-4312-2623			
Email: FBU.Paris@ssa.gov			

Cabo Verde	Cameroon	Canada

Federal Benefits Unit
United States Embassy
Avenida das Forcas
  Armadas
1600 Lisbon
Portugal
Phone: 351-2172-73300
Fax: 351-2172-68696
Email: FBU.Lisbon@ssa.gov
	Federal Benefits Unit
	United States Embassy
	4 Avenue Gabriel
	75382 Paris Cedex 08
	France
	Phone: 331-4312-2705
	Fax: 331-4312-2623
	Email: FBU.Paris@ssa.gov
		Resident Office for those
		  residing in
		Canada please click link
		  below
		Canadian Service Area
		  Directory
		https://www.ssa.gov
		  /foreign/canada.htm
		
		Residents of Ontario,
		  Canada click this link:
		https://www.ssa.gov
		  /foreign/ontario.htm
		Ontario, Canada

Cambodia	**Central African Republic**	**Chile**

Federal Benefits Unit
United States Embassy
1201 Roxas Boulevard
Ermita, Manila 0930
Philippines
Phone: 632-5301-2000
Fax: 632-8708-9714 or
  632-8708-9723
Email: FBU.Manila@ssa.gov
	Federal Benefits Unit
	United States Embassy
	4 Avenue Gabriel
	75382 Paris Cedex 08
	France
	Phone: 331-4312-2705
	Fax: 331-4312-2623
	Email: FBU.Paris@ssa.gov
		Federal Benefits Unit
		United States Embassy
		Calle 120 Avenida 0
		Pavas 1200
		San Jose
		Costa Rica
		Phone: 506-2519-2228
		Fax: 506-2291-1032
		Email: FBU.CostaRica
		  @ssa.gov

Cayman Islands	**Chad**	
Federal Benefits Unit United States Embassy Av. Republica de Colombia # 57 Santo Domingo Dominican Republic Phone: 809-368-7011 Fax: 809-368-7854 Email: FBU.Santo. Domingo@ssa.gov	Federal Benefits Unit United States Embassy 4 Avenue Gabriel 75382 Paris Cedex 08 France Phone: 331-4312-2705 Fax: 331-4312-2623 Email: FBU.Paris@ssa.gov	

China
Federal Benefits Unit
United States Embassy
1201 Roxas Boulevard
Ermita, Manila 0930
Philippines
Phone: 632-5301-2000
Fax: 632-8708-9714 or
632-8708-9723
Email: FBU.Manila@ssa.gov

Congo Kinshasa (DRC)
Federal Benefits Unit
United States Embassy
4 Avenue Gabriel
75382 Paris Cedex 08
France
Phone: 331-4312-2705
Fax: 331-4312-2623
Email: FBU.Paris@ssa.gov

Colombia
Federal Benefits Unit
United States Embassy
Av. Republica de Colombia
#57
Santo Domingo
Dominican Republic
Phone: 809-368-7011
Fax: 809-368-7854
Email: FBU.Santo.
   Domingo@ssa.gov

Costa Rica
Federal Benefits Unit
United States Embassy
Calle 120 Avenida 0
Pavas 1200
San Jose
Costa Rica
Phone: 506-2519-2228
Fax: 506-2291-1032
Email: FBU.CostaRica
   @ssa.gov

Comoros
Federal Benefits Unit
United States Embassy
91 Vasilisis Sophias Avenue
101 60 Athens
Greece
Phone: 302-1072-02426 or
302-1072-02412
Fax: 302-1064-69885
Email: FBU.Athens@ssa.gov

Côte d'Ivoire
Federal Benefits Unit
United States Embassy
4 Avenue Gabriel
75382 Paris Cedex 08
France
Phone: 331-4312-2705
Fax: 331-4312-2623
Email: FBU.Paris@ssa.gov

Congo Brazzaville
Federal Benefits Unit
United States Embassy
4 Avenue Gabriel
75382 Paris Cedex 08
France
Phone: 331-4312-2705
Fax: 331-4312-2623
Email: FBU.Paris@ssa.gov

Croatia
Federal Benefits Unit
United States Embassy
91 Vasilisis Sophias Avenue
101 60 Athens
Greece
Phone: 302-1072-02426 or
302-1072-02412
Fax: 302-1064-69885
Email: FBU.Athens@ssa.gov

Cuba Federal Benefits Unit United States Embassy Av. Republica de Colombia #57 Santo Domingo Dominican Republic Phone: 809-368-7011 Fax: 809-368-7854 Email: FBU.Santo.Domingo@ssa.gov	**Curacao** Federal Benefits Unit United States Embassy Av. Republica de Colombia #57 Santo Domingo Dominican Republic Phone: 809-368-7011 Fax: 809-368-7854 Email: FBU.Santo.Domingo@ssa.gov
Cyprus Federal Benefits Unit United States Embassy 91 Vasilisis Sophias Avenue 101 60 Athens Greece Phone: 302-1072-02426 or 302-1072-02412 Fax: 302-1064-69885 Email: FBU.Athens@ssa.gov	**Diego Garcia** Federal Benefits Unit United States Embassy 91 Vasilisis Sophias Avenue 101 60 Athens Greece Phone: 302-1072-02426 or 302-1072-02412 Fax: 302-1064-69885 Email: FBU.Athens@ssa.gov
Czech Republic Federal Benefits Unit United States Embassy ul. Piekna 12 00–539 Warsaw Poland Fax: 48-22-504-2281 Email: FBU.Warsaw@ssa.gov	**Denmark** Federal Benefits Unit United States Embassy PO Box 4075 AMB 0244 Oslo Norway Phone: 472-130-8540 Fax: 472-255-2743 Email: FBU.Oslo@ssa.gov
Djibouti Federal Benefits Unit United States Embassy 4 Avenue Gabriel 75382 Paris Cedex 08 France Phone: 331-4312-2705 Fax: 331-4312-2623 Email: FBU.Paris@ssa.gov	**Dominica** Federal Benefits Unit United States Embassy Av. Republica de Colombia #57 Santo Domingo Dominican Republic Phone: 809-368-7011 Fax: 809-368-7854 Email: FBU.Santo.Domingo@ssa.gov

Dominican Republic Federal Benefits Unit United States Embassy Av. Republica de Colombia # 57 Santo Domingo Dominican Republic Phone: 809-368-7011 Fax: 809-368-7854 Email: FBU.Santo.Domingo@ssa.gov	**Equatorial Guinea** Federal Benefits Unit United States Embassy Serrano 75 28006 Madrid Spain Phone: 349-1587-2261 Fax: 349-1587-2260 Email: FBU.Madrid@ssa.gov
Ecuador Federal Benefits Unit United States Embassy Av. Republica de Colombia #57 Santo Domingo Dominican Republic Phone: 809-368-7011 Fax: 809-368-7854 Email: FBU.Santo.Domingo@ssa.gov	**El Salvador** Federal Benefits Unit United States Embassy Calle 120 Avenida 0 Pavas 1200 San Jose Costa Rica Phone: 506-2519-2228 Fax: 506-2291-1032 Email: FBU.CostaRica@ssa.gov
Egypt Federal Benefits Unit United States Consulate General Piazza della Repubblica 80122 Naples Italy Inquiries/Contact: https://it.usembassy.gov/u-s-citizen-services/fbu/fbu-naples-inquiry-form/ Fax: 39-081-761-1804	

Eritrea Federal Benefits Unit United States Embassy Via Veneto 119 / A 00187 Rome Italy Inquiries/Contact: https: //it.usembassy.gov/u-s -citizen-services/fbu /fbu-rome-inquiry-form/ Fax: 39-06-4674-2542	**Ethiopia** Federal Benefits Unit United States Embassy Via Veneto 119 / A 00187 Rome Italy Inquiries/Contact: https: //it.usembassy.gov/u-s -citizen-services/fbu/ fbu-rome-inquiry-form/ Fax: 39-06-4674-2542
Estonia Federal Benefits Unit United States Embassy ul. Piekna 12 00–539 Warsaw Poland Fax: 48-22-504-2281 Email: FBU.Warsaw@ssa. gov	**France** Federal Benefits Unit United States Embassy 4 Avenue Gabriel 75382 Paris Cedex 08 France Phone: 331-4312-2705 Fax: 331-4312-2623 Email: FBU.Paris@ssa.gov
Fiji Federal Benefits Unit United States Embassy 1201 Roxas Boulevard Ermita, Manila 0930 Philippines Phone: 632-5301-2000 Fax: 632-8708-9714 or 632-8708-9723 Email: FBU.Manila@ssa.gov	**Finland** Federal Benefits Unit United States Embassy PO Box 4075 AMB 0244 Oslo Norway Phone: 472-130-8540 Fax: 472-255-2743 Email: FBU.Oslo@ssa.gov
	French Polynesia Federal Benefits Unit United States Embassy 1201 Roxas Boulevard Ermita, Manila 0930 Philippines Phone: 632-5301-2000 Fax: 632-8708-9714 or 632-8708-9723 Email: FBU.Manila@ssa.gov

Gabon
Federal Benefits Unit
United States Embassy
4 Avenue Gabriel
75382 Paris Cedex 08
France
Phone: 331-4312-2705
Fax: 331-4312-2623
Email: FBU.Paris@ssa.gov

Gambia
Federal Benefits Unit
United States Embassy
33 Nine Elms Lane
London
SW11 7US
Phone: 44-207-499-9000
  (10:00 – 1:00)
Fax: 44-207-891-3631
Email: FBU.London@ssa.gov

Gaza
Federal Benefits Unit
United States Embassy
14 David Flosser Street
Jerusalem 91002
Phone: 972-2630-4031
Fax: 972-2630-4147
Email: FBU.Jerusalem@ssa.gov

Georgia
Federal Benefits Unit
United States Embassy
91 Vasilisis Sophias Avenue
101 60 Athens
Greece
Phone: 302-1072-02426 or
302-1072-02412
Fax: 302-1064-69885
Email: FBU.Athens@ssa.gov

Germany
Federal Benefits Unit
United States Consulate
  General
Giessener Strasse 30
60435 Frankfurt
Germany
Phone: 49-69-90555-1100
Fax: 49-69-749352
Email: FBU.Frankfurt@ssa.gov

Ghana
Federal Benefits Unit
United States Embassy
33 Nine Elms Lane
London
SW11 7US
Phone: 44-207-499-9000
  (10:00 – 1:00)
Fax: 44-207-495-891-3631
Email: FBU.London@ssa.gov

Gibraltar
Federal Benefits Unit
United States Embassy
Serrano 75
28006 Madrid
Spain
Phone: 349-1587-2261
Fax: 349-1587-2260
Email: FBU.Madrid@ssa.gov

Greece
Federal Benefits Unit
American Embassy
91 Vasilisis Sophias Avenue
101 60 Athens
Greece
Phone: 302-1072-02426 or
302-1072-02412
Fax: 302-1064-69885
Email: FBU.Athens@ssa.gov

Greenland
Federal Benefits Unit
United States Embassy
PO Box 4075 AMB
0244 Oslo
Norway
Phone: 472-130-8540
Fax: 472-255-2743
Email: FBU.Oslo@ssa.gov

Grenada
Federal Benefits Unit
United States Embassy
Av. Republica de Colombia
57
Santo Domingo
Dominican Republic
Phone: 809-368-7011
Fax: 809-368-7854
Email: FBU.Santo.
Domingo@ssa.gov

Guadeloupe
Federal Benefits Unit
United States Embassy
Av. Republica de Colombia
#57
Santo Domingo
Dominican Republic
Phone: 809-368-7011
Fax: 809-368-7854
Email: FBU.Santo.
Domingo@ssa.gov

Guatemala
Federal Benefits Unit
United States Embassy
Calle 120 Avenida 0
Pavas 1200
San Jose
Costa Rica
Phone: 506-2519-2228
Fax: 506-2291-1032
Email: FBU.CostaRica
@ssa.gov

Guinea
Federal Benefits Unit
United States Embassy
4 Avenue Gabriel
75382 Paris Cedex 08
France
Phone: 331-4312-2705
Fax: 331-4312-2623
Email: FBU.Paris@ssa.gov

Guinea Bissau
Federal Benefits Unit
United States Embassy
Avenida das Forcas
Armadas
1600 Lisbon
Portugal
Phone: 351-2172-73300
Fax: 351-2172-68696
Email: FBU.Lisbon@ssa.gov

Guyana
Federal Benefits Unit
United States Embassy
Av. Republica de Colombia
57
Santo Domingo
Dominican Republic
Phone: 809-368-7011
Fax: 809-368-7854
Email: FBU.Santo.
Domingo@ssa.gov

Hungary Federal Benefits Unit United States Consulate General ul. Stolarska 9 31-043 Krakow Poland Fax: 48-12-424-5120 Email: FBU.Krakow@ssa.gov	**Iran** Federal Benefits Unit United States Consulate General Giessener Strasse 30 60435 Frankfurt Germany Phone: 49-69-90555-1100 Fax: 49-69-749352 Email: FBU.Frankfurt@ssa .gov
Hong Kong Federal Benefits Unit United States Embassy 1201 Roxas Boulevard Ermita, Manila 0930 Philippines Phone: 632-5301-2000 Fax: 632-8708-9714 or 632-8708-9723 Email: FBU.Manila@ssa.gov	**Indonesia** Federal Benefits Unit United States Embassy 1201 Roxas Boulevard Ermita, Manila 0930 Philippines Phone: 632-5301-2000 Fax: 632-8708-9714 or 632-8708-9723 Email: FBU.Manila@ssa.gov
Honduras Federal Benefits Unit United States Embassy Calle 120 Avenida 0 Pavas 1200 San Jose Costa Rica Phone: 506-2519-2228 Fax: 506-2291-1032 Email: FBU.CostaRica @ssa.gov	**India** Federal Benefits Unit United States Embassy 1201 Roxas Boulevard Ermita, Manila 0930 Philippines Phone: 632-5301-2000 Fax: 632-8708-9714 or 632-8708-9723 Email: FBU.Manila@ssa.gov
Haiti Federal Benefits Unit United States Embassy Av. Republica de Colombia #57 Santo Domingo Dominican Republic Phone: 809-368-7011 Fax: 809-368-7854 Email: FBU.Santo. Domingo@ssa.gov	**Iceland** Federal Benefits Unit United States Embassy PO Box 4075 AMB 0244 Oslo Norway Phone: 472-130-8540 Fax: 472-255-2743 Email: FBU.Oslo@ssa.gov

Iraq	Ireland	Israel	Italy
Federal Benefits Unit	Federal Benefits Unit	Federal Benefits Unit	The office below that
United States Embassy	United States Embassy	United States Embassy	is nearest to you:
Via Veneto 119/A	42 Elgin Road	14 David Flosser Street	Federal Benefits Unit
00187 Rome	Ballsbridge	Jerusalem 91002	United States Consulate
Italy	Dublin 4	Israel	General
Inquiries/Contact: https:	Ireland	Phone: 972-2630-4031	Piazza della Repubblica
//it.usembassy.gov/u-s	Phone: 353-1668-8777	Fax: 972-2630-4147	80122 Naples
-citizen-services/fbu	Ext: 2112	Email: FBUJerusalem@ssa	Italy
/fbu-rome-inquiry-form/	(Mornings Only)	.gov	Inquiries/Contact: https:
Fax: 39-06-4674-2542	Fax: 353-1668-7245		//it.usembassy.gov/u-s
	Email: FBU.Dublin@ssa.gov		-citizen-services/fbu
			/fbu-naples-inquiry-form/
			Fax: 39-081-7611804
			Federal Benefits Unit
			United States Embassy
			Via Veneto 119 / A
			00187 Rome
			Italy
			Inquiries/Contact: https:
			//it.usembassy.gov/u-s
			-citizen-services/fbu
			/fbu-rome-inquiry-form/
			Fax: 39-06-4674-2542

Jamaica
Federal Benefits Unit
United States Embassy
Av. Republica de Colombia
57
Santo Domingo
Dominican Republic
Phone: 809-368-7011
Fax: 809-368-7854
Email: FBU.Santo.
   Domingo@ssa.gov

Japan
Federal Benefits Unit
United States Embassy
1-10-5 Akasaka
Minato-ku
Tokyo 107-8420
Japan
Phone: 813-3224-5000
Fax: 813-3224-5144
Email: FBU.Tokyo@ssa.gov

Jerusalem
Federal Benefits Unit
United States Embassy
14 David Flosser Street
Jerusalem 91002
Phone: 972-2630-4031
Fax: 972-2630-4147
Email: FBU.Jerusalem@ssa
.gov

Jordan
Federal Benefits Unit
United States Consulate
   General
Piazza della Repubblica
80122 Naples
Italy
Inquiries/Contact: https:
//it.usembassy.gov/u-s
-citizen-services/fbu
/fbu-naples-inquiry-form/
Fax: 39-081-761-1804

Kazakhstan
Federal Benefits Unit
United States Embassy
91 Vasilisis Sophias Avenue
101 60 Athens
Greece
Phone: 302-1072-02426 or
302-1072-02412
Fax: 302-1064-69885
Email: FBU.Athens@ssa.gov

Kenya
Federal Benefits Unit
United States Embassy
33 Nine Elms Lane
London
SW11 7US
Phone: 44-207-499-9000
   (10:00 - 1:00)
Fax: 44-207-891-3631
   Email: FBU.London
   @ssa.gov

Kiribati
Federal Benefits Unit
United States Embassy
1201 Roxas Boulevard
Ermita, Manila 0930
Philippines
Phone: 632-5301-2000
Fax: 632-8708-9714 or
   632-8708-9723
Email: FBU.Manila@ssa.gov

Korea, North
Federal Benefits Unit
United States Embassy
1201 Roxas Boulevard
Ermita, Manila 0930
Philippines
Phone: 632-5301-2000
Fax: 632-8708-9714 or
   632-8708-9723
Email: FBU.Manila@ssa.gov

Korea, South	
Federal Benefits Unit United States Embassy 1201 Roxas Boulevard Ermita, Manila 0930 Philippines Phone: 632-5301-2000 Fax: 632-8708-9714 or 632-8708-9723 Email: FBU.Manila@ssa.gov	
Kuwait Federal Benefits Unit United States Embassy Via Veneto 119/A 00187 Rome Italy Inquiries/Contact: https:// it.usembassy.gov/u-s-citizen-services/fbu/ fbu-rome-inquiry-form/ Fax: 39-06-4674-2542	**Kyrgyzstan** Federal Benefits Unit United States Embassy 91 Vasilisis Sophias Avenue 101 60 Athens Greece Phone: 302-1072-02426 or 302-1072-02412 Fax: 302-1064-69885 Email: FBU.Athens@ssa.gov
Kosovo Federal Benefits Unit United States Embassy 91 Vasilisis Sophias Avenue 101 60 Athens Greece Phone: 302-1072-02426 or 302-1072-02412 Fax: 302-1064-69885 Email: FBU.Athens@ssa.gov	

Laos	Latvia	Lebanon	Lesotho
Federal Benefits Unit United States Embassy 1201 Roxas Boulevard Ermita, Manila 0930 Philippines Phone: 632-5301-2000 Fax: 632-8708-9714 or 632-8708-9723 Email: FBU.Manila@ssa.gov	Federal Benefits Unit United States Embassy ul. Piekna 12 00–539 Warsaw Poland Fax: 48-22-504-2281 Email: FBU.Warsaw@ssa.gov	Federal Benefits Unit United States Embassy Via Veneto 119/A 00187 Rome Italy Inquiries/Contact: https://it.usembassy.gov/u-s-citizen-services/fbu/fbu-rome-inquiry-form/ Fax: 39-06-4674-2542	Federal Benefits Unit United States Embassy 33 Nine Elms Lane London SW 11 7US Phone: 44-207-499-9000 (10:00 – 1:00) Fax: 44-207-891-3631 Email: FBU.London@ssa.gov
Liberia Federal Benefits Unit United States Embassy 33 Nine Elms Lane London SW 11 7US Phone: 44-207-499-9000 (10:00 – 1:00) Fax: 44-207-891-3631 Email: FBU.London@ssa.gov	**Libya** Federal Benefits Unit United States Embassy Via Veneto 119 / A 00187 Rome Italy Inquiries/Contact: https://it.usembassy.gov/u-s-citizen-services/fbu/fbu-rome-inquiry-form/ Fax: 39-06-4674-2542	**Liechtenstein** Federal Benefits Unit United States Consulate General Giessener Strasse 30 60435 Frankfurt Germany Phone: 49-69-90555-1100 Fax: 49-69-749352 Email: FBU.Frankfurt@ssa.gov	**Lithuania** Federal Benefits Unit United States Embassy ul. Piekna 12 00–539 Warsaw Poland Fax: 48-22-504-2281 Email: FBU.Warsaw@ssa.gov

		Madagascar	Malawi
		Federal Benefits Unit	Federal Benefits Unit
		United States Embassy	United States Embassy
		4 Avenue Gabriel	33 Nine Elms Lane
		75382 Paris Cedex 08	London
		France	SW11 7US
		Phone: 331–4312–2705	Phone: 44-207-499-9000
		Fax: 331–4312–2623	(10:00 – 1:00)
		Email: FBU.Paris@ssa.gov	Fax: 44-207-891-3631
			Email: FBU.London@ssa.gov
Luxembourg	**Macedonia**		
Federal Benefits Unit	Federal Benefits Unit		
United States Embassy	United States Consulate		
42 Elgin Road	General		
Ballsbridge	Piazza della Repubblica		
Dublin 4	80122 Naples		
Ireland	Italy		
Phone: 353–1668–8777	Inquiries/Contact: https:		
Ext: 2112	//it.usembassy.gov/u-s		
(Mornings Only)	-citizen-services/fbu		
Fax: 353–1668–7245	/fbu-naples-inquiry-form/		
FBU.Dublin@ssa.gov	Fax: 39-081-761-1804		
Macau			
Federal Benefits Unit			
United States Embassy			
1201 Roxas Boulevard			
Ermita, Manila 0930			
Philippines			
Phone: 632-5301-2000			
Fax: 632-8708-9714 or			
632-8708-9723			
Email: FBU.Manila@ssa.gov			

Malaysia
Federal Benefits Unit
United States Embassy
1201 Roxas Boulevard
Ermita, Manila 0930
Philippines
Phone: 632-5301-2000
Fax: 632-8708-9714 or
   632-8708-9723
Email: FBU.Manila@ssa.gov

Maldives
Federal Benefits Unit
United States Embassy
1201 Roxas Boulevard
Ermita, Manila 0930
Philippines
Phone: 632-5301-2000
Fax: 632-8708-9714 or
   632-8708-9723
Email: FBU.Manila@ssa.gov

Mali
Federal Benefits Unit
United StatesEmbassy
Federal Benefits Unit
4 Avenue Gabriel
75382 Paris Cedex 08
France
Phone: 331-4312-2705
Fax: 331-4312-2623
Email: FBU.Paris@ssa.gov

Malta
Federal Benefits Unit
United States Embassy
Via Veneto 119 / A
00187 Rome
Italy
Inquiries/Contact: https:
//it.usembassy.gov/u-s
-citizen-services/fbu
/fbu-rome-inquiry-form/
Fax: 39-06-4674-2542

Marshall Islands
Federal Benefits Unit
United States Embassy
1201 Roxas Boulevard
Ermita, Manila 0930
Philippines
Phone: 632-5301-2000
Fax: 632-8708-9714 or
   632-8708-9723
Email: FBU.Manila@ssa.gov

Martinique
Federal Benefits Unit
United States Embassy
Av. Republica de Colombia
57
Santo Domingo
Dominican Republic
Phone: 809-368-7011
Fax: 809-368-7854
Email: FBU.Santo.
   Domingo@ssa.gov

Mauritania
Federal Benefits Unit
United States Embassy
4 Avenue Gabriel
75382 Paris Cedex 08
France
Phone: 331-4312-2705
Fax: 331-4312-2623
Email: FBU.Paris@ssa.gov

Mauritius
Federal Benefits Unit
United States Embassy
91 Vasilisis Sophias Avenue
101 60 Athens
Greece
Phone: 302-1072-02426 or
302-1072-02412
Fax: 302-1064-69885
Email: FBU.Athens@ssa.gov

Mexico	Micronesia	Moldova	Monaco
The office below that is nearest to you:	Federal Benefits Unit	Federal Benefits Unit	Federal Benefits Unit
	United States Embassy	United States Embassy	United States Embassy
Federal Benefits Unit	1201 Roxas Boulevard	91 Vasilisis Sophias Avenue	4 Avenue Gabriel
United States Consulate General	Ermita, Manila 0930	101 60 Athens	75382 Paris Cedex 08
Paseo de la Victoria 3650	Philippines	Greece	France
32534 Ciudad Juarez, Chihuahua	Phone: 632-5301-2000	Phone: 302-1072-02426 or	Phone: 331-4312-2705
Mexico	Fax: 632-8708-9714 or	302-1072-02412	Fax: 331-4312-2623
Phone: 01-800-772-6394 (within Mexico only)	632-8708-9723	Fax: 302-1064-69885	Email: FBU.Paris@ssa.gov
Fax: 1-656-227-3501	Email: FBU.Manila@ssa.gov	Email: FBU.Athens@ssa.gov	
Email: FBU.Ciudad. Juarez@ssa.gov			
Federal Benefits Unit			
United States Consulate General			
Progreso 175			
44100 Guadalajara, Jalisco			
Mexico			
Phone: 01-800-772-6394 (within Mexico only)			
Fax: 52-33-3268-0803			
Email: FBU.Guadalajara@ ssa.gov			

(continued)

Federal Benefits Unit
United States Embassy
Paseo de la Reforma 305
06500 Mexico D. F.
Mexico
Phone: 01-800-772-6394
(within Mexico only) or
052-55-1102-6300
Fax: 052-55-1102-6301
Email: FBU.Mexico.City@ssa.gov

Mongolia
Federal Benefits Unit
United States Embassy
1201 Roxas Boulevard
Ermita, Manila 0930
Philippines
Phone: 632-5301-2000
Fax: 632-8708-9714 or
632-8708-9723
Email: FBU.Manila@ssa.gov

Montserrat
Federal Benefits Unit
United States Embassy
Av. Republica de Colombia
#57
Santo Domingo
Dominican Republic
Phone: 809-368-7011
Fax: 809-368-7854
Email: FBU.Santo.Domingo@ssa.gov

Montenegro
Federal Benefits Unit
United States Embassy
91 Vasilisis Sophias Avenue
101 60 Athens
Greece
Phone: 302-1072-02426 or
302-1072-02412
Fax: 302-1064-69885
Email: FBU.Athens@ssa.gov

Morocco
Federal Benefits Unit
United States Embassy
Federal Benefits Unit
4 Avenue Gabriel
75382 Paris Cedex 08
France
Phone: 331-4312-2705
Fax: 331-4312-2623
Email: FBU.Paris@ssa.gov

Mozambique
Federal Benefits Unit
United States Embassy
Avenida das Forcas
    Armadas
1600 Lisbon
Portugal
Phone: 351-2172-73300
Fax: 351-2172-68696
Email: FBU.Lisbon@ssa.gov

Namibia
Federal Benefits Unit
United States Embassy
33 Nine Elms Lane
London
SW11 7US
Phone: 44-207-499-9000
    (10:00 – 1:00)
Fax: 44-207-891-3631
Email: FBU.London@ssa.gov

Nauru
Federal Benefits Unit
United States Embassy
1201 Roxas Boulevard
Ermita, Manila 0930
Philippines
Ireland
Phone: 632-5301-2000
Fax: 632-8708-9714 or
    632-8708-9723
Email: FBU.Manila@ssa.gov

Nepal
Federal Benefits Unit
United States Embassy
1201 Roxas Boulevard
Ermita, Manila 0930
Philippines
Ireland
Phone: 632-5301-2000
Fax: 632-8708-9714 or
    632-8708-9723
Email: FBU.Manila@ssa.gov

Netherlands
Federal Benefits Unit
United States Embassy
42 Elgin Road
Ballsbridge
Dublin 4
Ireland
Phone: 353-1668-8777
    Ext: 2112
    (Mornings Only)
Fax: 353-1668-7245
Email: FBU.Dublin@ssa.gov

New Caledonia Federal Benefits Unit United States Embassy 1201 Roxas Boulevard Ermita, Manila 0930 Philippines Phone: 632-5301-2000 Fax: 632-8708-9714 or 632-8708-9723 Email: FBU.Manila@ssa.gov	**New Zealand** Fderal Benefits Unit United States Embassy 1201 Roxas Boulevard Ermita, Manila 0930 Philippines Phone: 632-5301-2000 Fax: 632-8708-9714 or 632-8708-9723 Email: FBU.Manila@ssa.gov	**Nicaragua** Federal Benefits Unit United States Embassy Calle 120 Avenida 0 Pavas 1200 San Jose Costa Rica Phone: 506-2519-2228 Fax: 506-2291-1032 Email: FBU.CostaRica @ssa.gov	**Niger** Federal Benefits Units United States Embassy 4 Avenue Gabriel 75382 Paris Cedex 08 France Phone: 331-4312-2705 Fax: 331-4312-2623 Email: FBU.Paris@ssa.gov
Nigeria Federal Benefits Unit United States Embassy 33 Nine Elms Lane London SW11 7US Phone: 44-207-499-9000 (10:00 - 1:00) Fax: 44-207-891-3631 Email: FBU.London @ssa.gov	**Norway** Federal Benefits Unit United States Embassy PO Box 4075 AMB 0244 Oslo Norway Phone: 472-130-8540 Fax: 472-255-2743 Email: FBU.Oslo@ssa.gov		

Oman Federal Benefits Unit United States Embassy Via Veneto 119/A 00187 Rome Italy Phone: Inquiries/Contact: https://it.usembassy.gov /u-s-citizen-services/fbu /fbu-rome-inquiry-form/ Fax: 39-06-4674-2542		
Pakistan Federal Benefits Unit United States Embassy 1201 Roxas Boulevard Ermita, Manila 0930 Philippines Phone: 632-5301-2000 Fax: 632-8708-9714 or 632-8708-9723 Email: FBU.Manila@ssa.gov	**Palau** Federal Benefits Unit United States Embassy 1201 Roxas Boulevard Ermita, Manila 0930 Philippines Phone: 632-5301-2000 Fax: 632-8708-9714 or 632-8708-9723 Email: FBU.Manila@ssa.gov	**Panama** Federal Benefits Unit United States Embassy Calle 120 Avenida 0 Pavas 1200 San Jose Costa Rica Phone: 506-2519-2228 Fax: 506-2291-1032 Email: FBU.CostaRica @ssa.gov
		Papua New Guinea Federal Benefits Unit United States Embassy 1201 Roxas Boulevard Ermita, Manila 0930 Philippines Phone: 632-5301-2000 Fax: 632-8708-9714 or 632-8708-9723 Email: FBU.Manila@ssa.gov

Paraguay	Peru	Philippines	Poland
Federal Benefits Unit	Federal Benefits Unit	Federal Benefits Unit	The office below that
United States Embassy	United States Embassy	United States Embassy	is nearest to you:
4300 Colombia	Calle 120 Avenida 0	1201 Roxas Boulevard	Federal Benefits Unit
1425 Buenos Aires	Pavas 1200	Ermita, Manila 0930	United States Consulate
Argentina	San Jose	Philippines	General
Phone: 5411-5777-4492	Costa Rica	Phone: 632-5301-2000	ul. Stolarska 9
Fax: 5411-5777-4231	Phone: 506-2519-2228	Fax: 632-8708-9714 or	31-043 Krakow
Email: FBU.Argentina	Fax: 506-2291-1032	632-8708-9723	Poland
@ssa.gov	Email: FBU.CostaRica	Email: FBU.Manila@ssa.gov	Fax: 48-12-424-5120
	@ssa.gov		Email: FBU.Krakow@ssa.gov
			Federal Benefits Unit
			United States Embassy
			ul. Piekna 12
			00-539 Warsaw
			Poland
			Fax: 48-22-504-2281
			Email: FBU.Warsaw@ssa.gov

Portugal
Federal Benefits Unit
United States Embassy
Avenida das Forcas
    Armadas
1600 Lisbon
Portugal
Phone: 351-2172-73300
Fax: 351-2172-68696
Email: FBU.Lisbon@ssa
    .gov

Qatar
Federal Benefits Unit
United States Embassy
Via Veneto 119/A
00187 Rome
Italy
Inquiries/Contact: https:
    //it.usembassy.gov/u-s
    -citizen-services/fbu
    /fbu-rome-inquiry-form/
Fax: 39-06-4674-2542

Saba
Federal Benefits Unit
United States Embassy
Av. Republica de Colombia
  # 57
Santo Domingo
Dominican Republic
Phone: 809-368-7011
Fax: 809-368-7854
Email: FBU.Santo.
  Domingo@ssa.gov
	Samoa
	Federal Benefits Unit
	United States Embassy
	1201 Roxas Boulevard
	Ermita, Manila 0930
	Philippines
	Phone: 632-5301-2000
	Fax: 632-8708-9714 or
	  632-8708-9723
	Email: FBUManila@ssa.gov

Sierra Leone
Federal Benefits Unit
United States Embassy
33 Nine Elms Lane
London
SW11 7US
Phone: 44-207-499-9000
  (10:00 – 1:00)
Fax: 44-207-891-3631
Email: FBU.London@ssa.gov
	Singapore
	Federal Benefits Unit
	United States Embassy
	1201 Roxas Boulevard
	Ermita, Manila 0930
	Philippines
	Phone: 632-5301-2000
	Fax: 632-8708-9714 or
	  632-8708-9723
	Email: FBUManila@ssa.gov

San Marino
Federal Benefits Unit
United States Embassy
Via Veneto 119 / A
00187 Rome
Italy
Inquiries/Contact: https:
  //it.usembassy.gov/u-s
  -citizen-services/fbu
  /fbu-rome-inquiry-form/
Fax: 39-06-4674-2542
	Sao Tome & Principe
	Federal Benefits Unit
	United States Embassy
	Avenida das Forcas
	  Armadas
	1600 Lisbon
	Portugal
	Phone: 351-2172-73300
	Fax: 351-2172-68696
	Email: FBU.Lisbon@ssa.gov

Slovakia
Federal Benefits Unit
United States Embassy
ul. Piekna 12
00–539 Warsaw
Poland
Fax: 48-22-504-2281
Email: FBUWarsaw@ssa.gov
	Slovenia
	Federal Benefits Unit
	United States Embassy
	Via Veneto 119/A
	00187 Rome
	Italy
	Inquiries/Contact: https:
	  //it.usembassy.gov/u-s
	  -citizen-services/fbu
	  /fbu-rome-inquiry-form/
	Fax: 39-06-4674-2542

Reunion	Republic of Congo	Romania	Russia
Federal Benefits Unit United States Embassy 4 Avenue Gabriel 75382 Paris Cedex 08 France Phone: 331-4312-2705 Fax: 331-4312-2623 Email: FBU.Paris@ssa.gov	Federal Benefits Unit United States Embassy 4 Avenue Gabriel 75382 Paris Cedex 08 France Phone: 331-4312-2705 Fax: 331-4312-2623 Email: FBU.Paris@ssa.gov	Federal Benefits Unit United States Consulate General Piazza della Repubblica 80122 Naples Italy Inquiries/Contact: https: //it.usembassy.gov/u-s -citizen-services/fbu /fbu-naples-inquiry-form/ Fax: 39-081-761-1804	Federal Benefits Unit United States Embassy ul. Piekna 12 00-539 Warsaw Poland Fax: 48-22-504-2281 Email: FBU.Warsaw@ssa.gov
Rwanda Federal Benefits Unit United States Embassy 4 Avenue Gabriel 75382 Paris Cedex 08 France Phone: 331-4312-2705 Fax: 331-4312-2623 Email: FBU.Paris@ssa.gov			

Soloman Islands
Federal Benefits Unit
United States Embassy
1201 Roxas Boulevard
Ermita, Manila 0930
Philippines
Phone: 632-5301-2000
Fax: 632-8708-9714 or
632-8708-9723
Email: FBU.Manila@ssa.gov

Spain
Federal Benefits Unit
United States Embassy
Serrano 75
28006 Madrid
Spain
Phone: 349-1587-2261
Fax: 349-1587-2260
Email: FBU.Madrid@ssa.gov

Somalia
Federal Benefits Unit
United States Embassy
33 Nine Elms Lane
London
SW11 7US
Phone: 44-207-499-9000
(10:00 - 1:00) Fax:
44-207-891-3631
Email: FBU.London@ssa.gov

Sri Lanka
Federal Benefits Unit
United States Embassy
1201 Roxas Boulevard
Ermita, Manila 0930
Philippines
Phone: 632-5301-2000
Fax: 632-8708-9714 or
632-8708-9723
Email: FBU.Manila@ssa.gov

South Africa
Federal Benefits Unit
United States Embassy
33 Nine Elms Lane
London
SW11 7US
Phone: 44-207-499-9000
(10:00 - 1:00)
Fax: 44-207-891-3631
Email: FBU.London@ssa.gov

**St. Helena &
Dependencies**
Federal Benefits Unit
United States Embassy
91 Vasilisis Sophias Avenue
101 60 Athens
Greece
Phone: 302-1072-02426 or
302-1072-02412
Fax: 302-1064-69885
Email: FBU.Athens@ssa.gov

South Sudan
Federal Benefits Unit
United States Embassy
Via Veneto 119/A
00187 Rome
Italy
Inquiries/Contact: https:
//it.usembassy.gov/u-s
-citizen-services/fbu
/fbu-rome-inquiry-form/
Fax: 39-06-4674-2542

St. Lucia
Federal Benefits Unit
United States Embassy
Av. Republica de Colombia
57
Santo Domingo
Dominican Republic
Phone: 809-368-7011
Fax: 809-368-7854
Email: FBU.Santo.
Domingo@ssa.gov

St. Nevis / Portola / St. Barthelemy
Federal Benefits Unit
United States Embassy
Av. Republica de Colombia
57
Santo Domingo
Dominican Republic
Phone: 809-368-7011
Fax: 809-368-7854
Email: FBU.Santo.
  Domingo@ssa.gov

Sudan
Federal Benefits Unit
United States Embassy
Via Veneto 119/A
00187 Rome
Italy
Inquiries/Contact: https:
//it.usembassy.gov/u-s
-citizen-services/fbu
/fbu-rome-inquiry-form/
Fax:39-06-4674-2542

St. Vincent & Grenadines
Federal Benefits Unit
United States Embassy
Av. Republica de Colombia
57
Santo Domingo
Dominican Republic
Phone: 809-368-7011
Fax: 809-368-7854
Email: FBU.Santo.
  Domingo@ssa.gov

Suriname
Federal Benefits Unit
United States Embassy
Av. Republica de Colombia
57
Santo Domingo
Dominican Republic
Phone: 809-368-7011
Fax: 809-368-7854
Email: FBU.Santo.
  Domingo@ssa.gov

Sint Eustatius
Federal Benefits Unit
United States Embassy
Av. Republica de Colombia
57
Santo Domingo
Dominican Republic
Phone: 809-368-7011
Fax: 809-368-7854
Email: FBU.Santo.
  Domingo@ssa.gov

Swaziland
Federal Benefits Unit
United States Embassy
33 Nine Elms Lane
London
SW11 7US
Phone: 44-207-499-9000
  (10:00 – 1:00)
Fax: 44-207-891-3631
Email: FBU.London@ssa.gov

Sint Maarten
Federal Benefits Unit
United States Embassy
Av. Republica de Colombia
57
Santo Domingo
Dominican Republic
Phone: 809-368-7011
Fax: 809-368-7854
Email: FBU.Santo.
  Domingo@ssa.gov

Sweden
Federal Benefits Unit
United States Embassy
PO Box 4075 AMB
0244 Oslo
Norway
Phone: 472-130-8540
Fax: 472-255-2743
Email: FBU.Oslo@ssa.gov

Switzerland
Federal Benefits Unit
United States Consulate General
Giessener Strasse 30
60435 Frankfurt
Germany
Phone: 49-69-90555-1100
Fax: 49-69-749352
Email: FBU.Frankfurt@ssa.gov

Syria
Federal Benefits Unit
United States Consulate General
Piazza della Repubblica
80122 Naples
Italy
Inquiries/Contact: https://it.usembassy.gov/u-s-citizen-services/fbu/fbu-naples-inquiry-form/
Fax: 39-081-761-1804

Tahiti
Federal Benefits Unit
United States Embassy
1201 Roxas Boulevard
Ermita, Manila 0930
Philippines
Phone: 632-5301-2000
Fax: 632-8708-9714 or 632-8708-9723
Email: FBU.Manila@ssa.gov

Taiwan
Federal Benefits Unit
United States Embassy
1201 Roxas Boulevard
Ermita, Manila 0930
Philippines
Phone: 632-5301-2000
Fax: 632-8708-9714 or 632-8708-9723
Email: FBU.Manila@ssa.gov

Tajikistan
Federal Benefits Unit
United States Embassy
91 Vasilisis Sophias Avenue
101 60 Athens
Greece
Phone: 302-1072-02426 or 302-1072-02412
Fax: 302-1064-69885
Email: FBU.Athens@ssa.gov

Tanzania
Federal Benefits Unit
United States Embassy
33 Nine Elms Lane
London
SW11 7US
Phone: 44-207-499-9000 (10:00 - 1:00)
Fax: 44-207-891-3631
Email: FBU.London@ssa.gov

Thailand
Federal Benefits Unit
United States Embassy
1201 Roxas Boulevard
Ermita, Manila 0930
Philippines
Phone: 632-5301-2000
Fax: 632-8708-9714 or
632-8708-9723
Email: FBU.Manila@ssa.gov

Timor-Leste (East Timor)
Federal Benefits Unit
United States Embassy
1201 Roxas Boulevard
Ermita, Manila 0930
Philippines
Phone: 632-5301-2000
Fax: 632-8708-9714 or
632-8708-9723
Email: FBU.Manila@ssa.gov

Togo
Federal Benefits Unit
United States Embassy
4 Avenue Gabriel
75382 Paris Cedex 08
France
Phone: 331-4312-2705
Fax: 331-4312-2623
Email: FBU.Paris@ssa.gov

Turkmenistan
Federal Benefits Unit
United States Embassy
91 Vasilisis Sophias Avenue
101 60 Athens
Greece
Phone: 302-1072-02426 or
302-1072-02412
Fax: 302-1064-69885
Email: FBU.Athens@ssa.gov

Trinidad & Tobago
Federal Benefits Unit
United States Embassy
Av. Republica de Colombia
57
Santo Domingo
Dominican Republic
Phone: 809-368-7011
Fax: 809-368-7854
Email: FBU.Santo.
Domingo@ssa.gov

Tunisia
Federal Benefits Unit
United States Embassy
4 Avenue Gabriel
75382 Paris Cedex 08
France
Phone: 331-4312-2705
Fax: 331-4312-2623
Email: FBU.Paris@ssa.gov

Turkey
Federal Benefits Unit
United States Embassy
91 Vasilisis Sophias Avenue
101 60 Athens
Greece
Phone: 302-1072-02426 or
302-1072-02412
Fax: 302-1064-69885
Email: FBU.Athens@ssa.gov

Turks & Caicos Islands	Tuvalu
Federal Benefits Unit	Federal Benefits Unit
United States Embassy	United States Embassy
Av. Republica de Colombia # 57	1201 Roxas Boulevard
	Ermita, Manila 0930
Santo Domingo	Philippines
Dominican Republic	Phone: 632-5301-2000
Phone: 809-368-7011	Fax: 632-8708-9714 or
Fax: 809-368-7854	632-8708-9723
Email: FBU.Santo. Domingo@ssa.gov	Email: FBU.Manila@ssa.gov
Uganda	**Ukraine**
Federal Benefits Unit	Federal Benefits Unit
United States Embassy	United States Embassy
33 Nine Elms Lane	ul. Piekna 12
London	00-539 Warsaw
SW11 7US	Poland
Phone: 44-207-499-9000 (10:00 – 1:00)	Fax: 48-22-504-2281
Fax: 44-207-891-3631	Email: FBU.Warsaw@ssa.gov
Email: FBU.London@ssa.gov	

United Arab Emirates	United Kingdom
Federal Benefits Unit	Federal Benefits Unit
United States Embassy	United States Embassy
Via Veneto 119/A	33 Nine Elms Lane
00187 Rome	London
Italy	SW11 7US
Inquiries/Contact: https://it.usembassy.gov/u-s-citizen-services/fbu/fbu-rome-inquiry-form/	Phone: 44-207-499-9000 (10:00 – 1:00)
Fax: 39-06-4674-2542	Fax: 44-207-891-3631
	Email: FBU.London @ssa.gov

Uruguay Federal Benefits Unit Unites States Embassy Calle 120 Avenida o Pavas 1200 San Jose Costa Rica Phone: 506-2519-2228 Fax: 506-2291-1032 Email: FBU.CostaRica@ssa.gov	**Uzbekistan** Federal Benefits Unit United States Embassy 91 Vasilisis Sophias Avenue 101 60 Athens Greece Phone: 302-1072-02426 or 302-1072-02412 Fax: 302-1064-69885 Email: FBU.Athens@ssa.gov
Vanuatu Federal Benefits Unit United States Embassy 1201 Roxas Boulevard Ermita, Manila 0930 Philippines Phone: 632-5301-2000 Fax: 632-8708-9714 or 632-8708-9723 Email: FBU.Manila@ssa.gov	**Venezuela** Federal Benefits Unit United States Embassy Calle 120 Avenida O Pavas 1200 San Jose Costa Rica Phone: 506-2519-2228 Fax: 506-2291-1032 Email: FBU.CostaRica@ ssa.gov
	Vietnam Federal Benefits Unit United States Embassy 1201 Roxas Boulevard Ermita, Manila 0930 Philippines Phone: 632-5301-2000 Fax: 632-8708-9714 or 632-8708-9723 Email: FBU.Manila@ssa.gov

West Bank Federal Benefits Unit United States Embassy 14 David Flosser Street Jerusalem 91002 Phone: 972-2630-4031 Fax: 972-2630-4147 Email: FBU.Jerusalem@ssa.gov	**Western Sahara** Federal Benefits Unit United States Embassy Serrano 75 28006 Madrid Spain Phone: 349-1587-2261 Fax: 349-1587-2260 Email: FBU.Madrid@ssa.gov
Yemen Federal Benefits Unit United States Embassy 91 Vasilisis Sophias Avenue 101 60 Athens Greece Phone: 302-1072-02426 or 302-1072-02412 Fax: 302-1064-69885 Email: FBU.Athens@ssa.gov	

Zambia	Zimbabwe
Federal Benefits Unit	Federal Benefits Unit
United States Embassy	United States Embassy
33 Nine Elms Lane	33 Nine Elms Lane
London	London
SW11 7US	SW11 7US
Phone: 44-207-499-9000	Phone: 44-207-499-9000
(10:00 – 1:00)	(10:00 – 1:00)
Fax: 44-207-891-3631	Fax: 44-207-891-3631
Email: FBU.London@ssa.gov	Email: FBU.London@ssa.gov

INDEX

Books from Allworth Press

Estate Planning (in Plain English)
by Leonard D. DuBoff and Amanda Bryan (6 × 9, 336 pages, paperback, $19.99)

Feng Shui and Money (Second Edition)
by Eric Shaffert (6 × 9, 256 pages, paperback, $19.99)

Help Yourself Now
by Jan Yager (6 x 9, 336 pages, paperback, $17.99)

How to Avoid Probate for Everyone
by Ronald Farrington Sharp (5½ × 8¼, 192 pages, paperback, $14.99)

How to Plan and Settle Estates
by Edmund Fleming (6 × 9, 288 pages, paperback, $16.95)

The Law (in Plain English)® for Small Business (Fifth Edition)
by Leonard D. DuBoff and Amanda Bryan (6 × 9, 312 pages, paperback, $24.99)

Legal Forms for Everyone (Sixth Edition)
by Carl Battle (8½ × 11, 280 pages, paperback, $24.99)

Living Trusts for Everyone (Second Edition)
by Ronald Farrington Sharp (5½ × 8¼, 192 pages, paperback $14.99)

Legal Guide to Social Media
by Kimberly A. Houser (6 × 9, 208 pages, paperback, $19.95)

Love & Money
by Ann-Margaret Carrozza with foreword by Dr. Phil McGraw (6 × 9, 240 pages, paperback, $19.99)

The Money Mentor
by Tad Crawford (6 × 9, 272 pages, paperback, $24.95)

Protecting Your Assets from Probate and Long-Term Care
by Evan H. Farr (6 × 9, 208 pages, paperback, $14.99)

Quadrant Life
by Lori Dennis with foreword by Farah Merhi (5.5 x 8.25, 216 pages, hardcover, $16.99)

Scammed
by Gini Graham Scott, PhD (6 × 9, 256 pages, paperback, $14.99)

The Secret Life of Money
by Tad Crawford (5½ × 8½, 304 pages, paperback, $19.95)

The Smart Consumer's Guide to Good Credit
by John Ulzheimer (5¼ × 8¼, 216 pages, paperback, $14.95)

To see our complete catalog or to order online, please visit *www.allworth.com*.